# A GUIDE TO BOTTLENECK SLIDE GUITAR

*By*
*Pete Madsen*

Cover photo by Teja Gerken
© 2014 Pete Madsen
All Rights Reserved
ISBN-9780615991405

www.learnbluesguitarnow.com

# A GUIDE TO BOTTLENECK SLIDE GUITAR

By
Pete Madsen

# A GUIDE TO BOTTLENECK SLIDE GUITAR

Welcome to *A Guide to Bottleneck Slide Guitar*! This book came about for a number of reasons. Originally, I had been asked by Backbeat Books to write a book about slide guitar in 2005 — you can still find that book on Amazon. At the time, I felt I was in over my head: what do I know about slide guitar? Sure, I have played some slide, and I thought I was pretty good at it, but writing an entire book on the subject?

 I did learn a lot writing that book and there are some good things in it — I have taken the liberty of reusing a few of those things here. But there is plenty of new stuff, including lots of new grooves, licks and tunings. Over the past nine years, as I have continued to teach and refine what I created in that book, I have learned some new skills and tunings related to slide, and so I realized that I had almost enough material for a new book on bottleneck slide.

 With a few additions and tweaks the culmination of that process is in your hands! or on your music stand.

 I have also just recently made some youtube videos to go along with the exercises and songs in the book. Some of the links are below. I will continue to add to these in the following months so keep checking back.


Terraplane Blues: http://www.youtube.com/watch?v=4Bav_YgfCTs


Death Letter Blues: http://www.youtube.com/watch?v=vHaeHWGFb-Q


Le Petit Nicolas: http://www.youtube.com/watch?v=c39N3oLavPw


Thanks and enjoy!
Pete
March 28 , 2014


www.learnbluesguitarnow.com

# CHAPTER 1:
## HISTORY
## AND BIOGRAPHIES

# *THE STORY*

In 1919, a 17-year-old Hawaiian boy named Solomon Ho'opi'i Ka'ai stowed away on an ocean liner bound for the United States. His dream was to make music for a living. He arrived in San Francisco and quickly moved to Los Angeles, where he formed a trio with Glenwood Leslie and Lani McIntyre. Little did Sol Hoopii know that the music he would end up recording in the years 1927-38, songs like 'Hula Blues,' 'Farewell Blues,' and 'Hawaiian March,' would influence a legion of guitar players from rural Mississippi, who in turn would influence another legion of guitarists decades later from across the Atlantic ocean. Hoopii did not invent slide guitar, but the popularity of these early Hawaiian 'slack key' guitar recordings would go on to be heard around the nation. The sound of a hard comb or steel bar being dragged across the strings had a haunting timbre that would creep into the souls of people around the world.

From its primitive beginnings to its maturity in the age of electric rock'n'roll, slide guitar has given the guitarist a voice that extends the emotional range of the instrument. The slide allowed guitarists to find the notes between notes; the place between the frets where the slippery quality of human emotion runs. The slide can make the strings growl or whimper; it can be bold and menacing or quiet and sympathetic. The slide can keep a run going, circling the perimeters of chord changes; or it could stop dead in its tracks and give the listener something to ponder.

Slide playing is personal; no two slide players sound alike. How can this be when everybody plays the same Robert Johnson riff? But so many variables, from heart to mind to physical approach, dictate how one plays that riff. I could play it and odds are when you play it back to me it will sound different. It's because we all hear something different in those notes between the notes, that space where the slide meets the string and is expressed by the individual in an infinite number of ways. Slide playing is elusive and alludes to something we can never fully capture in words.

So where did it come from, and who were the pioneers of slide?

EARLY HAWAIIAN SLIDE AND RESONATOR GUITARS

It is hard to pinpoint the origin of slide guitar. It really has several origins, including roots in Hawaii and West Africa. In Hawaii, during the 1800s, Portuguese and Mexican sailors introduced guitars to the native population. The Hawaiians adapted the guitar to their own style of music. They tuned the guitar to open chords, often by tuning the guitar 'down' or 'slackening' the strings. A knife blade, comb or bone would be dragged across the strings to produce a sustained glissando.

Joseph Kekeku is credited with inventing the Hawaiian style in the early 1880s. His recordings, along with those of later players such as Hoopii, Frank Ferera and Jim and Bob (The Genial Hawaiians), were well received and popular during the 1920s and early 1930s. It is said that before 1930 every Chinese restaurant, beer garden, and hotel had a Hawaiian band.

Hoopii was one of the first guitarists to popularize the steel guitar. The sound of the steel guitar, chillingly evocative, is what many people associate with the sound of early slide playing.

Manufactured by the Dopyera brothers, the National guitars were first conceived as a way for guitarists to compete in volume with a jazz band. The wood guitars of the era were not electrified and could hardly create the same volume as the brass or percussion instruments. These guitars were made of brass or steel, with an innovative 'resonator' design that amplified the sound of the strings by the use of a 'biscuit' (single cone) or 'T-bar' (Tricone) that transferred the vibration of the strings to something resembling a speaker cone(s). These guitars were not only loud, but when applying an open tuning and slide techniques to them produced an even more haunting and evocative sound than that of ordinary wood guitars; a sound that is most often associated with rural blues and such players as Charlie Patton, Son House and Tampa Red.

The National guitars (and later Dobro: a falling out between business partners led the Dopyera brothers to split off from National and form this new company) came in round and square neck versions. The square neck guitars were meant to be played on the lap, with the strings set far above the neck. These guitars were impossible to fret by conventional standards and were meant to be played strictly with a steel bar slid across the strings. To compensate for the inability to fret the guitar with their hands, square-neck players evolved several different tunings and techniques to allow them to play chords and melodies beyond major and minor triads. The square neck guitars evolved into what country players use today: the pedal steel guitar. The pedal steel is a form of lap-style guitar with as many as three separate necks.

The round neck Nationals, on the other hand, were meant to be played like a conventional guitar and thus became popular with many blues musicians. Tampa Red was the first blues artist to record with a National. His music was fairly sophisticated for a bluesman and his playing usually accompanied an orchestra or band. In contrast to Red were Son House, Charlie Patton and Bukka White, who played hard driving, primitive yet extremely evocative material that seemed to come from the earth itself.

Sol Ho'opi'i

Solomon Ho'opi'I Ka'ai'ai was born in 1902 in Honolulu, Hawaii, the youngest of 21 children. At an early age he began playing ukulele and soon brought the guitar and Hawaiian guitar into his instrumental repertoire. Hoopii's stowaway trip almost ended in disaster when he and his two companions were discovered on the boat, with the captain of the ship stymied because he couldn't kick the men off in the middle of the Pacific. The Hawaiian trio's answer was to charm the passengers with their music. The passengers were so elated they all pitched in to pay the trio's fare – or so the story goes.

Hoopii is considered the most influential Hawaiian guitarist of the 20th century. He also had considerable influence on Western Swing and Country pedal steel guitar, and, in as much as he was responsible for popularizing the National guitar, also an influence on blues artists of the day. (It was reciprocal, however; Hoopii also borrowed a lot from blues players.) When he performed songs like 'Hula Blues,' it was hard to deny the influence.

His group, The Sol Hoopii Novelty Trio, gained a certain amount of fame during the late 1920s as a performing and recording group. Their records were not only a hit nationally, but became international best-sellers. He was so popular at one point that he appeared in several Hollywood movies, including *Waikiki Wedding, Song of the Islands* and a few Charlie Chan movies. His playing also adorns the soundtrack to the Betty Boop cartoon *Betty's Bamboo Isle*.

Hoopii's earliest recording was in 1925 with The Waikiki Hawaiian Trio. His playing consisted mainly of rapid-fire single-string runs on a Lyon and Healy flat-top guitar. As his playing developed, he created even more complex chordal and melodic ideas. In 1935 he switched to lap steel guitar, using innovative tunings such as C# minor: B, D, E, G#, C#, E. The new tunings that he discovered opened up chordal and melodic possibilities that the standard Hawaiian tunings (open A or G) did not possess.

Songs: 'Hula Blues,' 'Farewell Blues'

BLUES SLIDE TRADITION

For centuries musicians in West Africa were using a bow-like instrument strung over a gourd and playing it over their stomachs. This instrument is still used in Africa today and is played by using an object, such as a bone, placed over the string and slid to alter the pitch. African slaves brought to America had very few possessions but were able to adapt and make versions of this instrument by nailing a piece of bailing wire to the floor or wall of a hut and sliding something, once again a bone or metal object, along the string. The early American version of this instrument was called a 'jitterbug.' There is also a version of this instrument that still exists today called the 'diddley bow.' Now you know where Bo Diddley got his name.

The Delta blues men were most likely aware of the recordings of the early Hawaiian players, but adapted their playing to their own style. For instance, instead of holding the guitar on their laps and playing a square neck guitar like the Hawaiian players, the blues players played the guitar in its standard position and used a conventional round neck guitar (except for the bluesman Black Ace, who played the square-neck variety of National guitar). Also, the Hawaiian players favored tunings such as open A (E, A, E, A, C#, E, low to high), E7 (E B G# D B E), or C# minor (B, D, E, G#, C#, E). The blues players favored open D (D, A, D, F#, A, D), open E (E, B, E, G#, B, E), or open G (D, G, D, G, B, E). While this may seem like a technical point, it is important to note that the relative pitches of the strings would affect how the player approached the instrument and the phrasings of what they played: the general characteristics of the music were bound not only by slide technique but how the player was able to navigate the fret board based on the guitar's tuning.

As the blues tradition evolved, the guitar became more prominent. It was the perfect instrument for the solo performer – infinitely more portable than a piano in rural Mississippi. It also had distinct advantages over the violin or banjo in that it was a better match for the human vocal register. A solo guitarist was welcome at a barn dance, parlors, or front porch jam session, where they would not only sing and play to the delight of the audience but were also expected to provide danceable tunes. Think about how hard it would be today for one person to not only entertain an audience but keep them dancing and you gain a new respect for these early blues guitarists.

As the playing evolved so did the slide. Originally knife blades and combs were used. It was the bluesmen who started to use tubes of metal, brass or glass – the best object being a broken or cut off top of a wine bottle. This allowed the player to put the slide over one finger and leave the others available for fretting chords and notes.

THE EARLY BLUES TRADITION

The music of the early bluesmen was not intended for a large audience, so it seems to have a deeply personal and resonant tone. As one can imagine, the rural south at the turn of the 20th century was wide open; there was lots of space and distances were not easily traveled. Nor was there much money to be made as a musician. Most of the musicians, including Robert Johnson and John Hurt, made their livings as farmers. In order to make money playing music, they would often have to travel to northern cities like Chicago, as Johnson sometimes did.

There was also a tradition of 'borrowing.' Players would use each other's licks and tricks, yet the ones we remember always gave the music their own personal stamp. The blues tradition was a folkloric tradition: passed down by word of mouth or sight of hand. It was and is not well served by modern recording techniques and studio trickery. We are fortunate that we have the early recordings of Johnson, Skip James, Bill Broonzy, Blind Willie McTell, Tampa Red, Blind Blake, Son House, Charlie Patton, Blind Lemon Jefferson, as a reminder of how truly innovative and great these players were.

Where blues comes from

Today the source of inspiration for most slide guitarists can be traced back to the blues artists of the early 20th century. To understand what the slide and blues evoke it is worth examining the cultural circumstances in which the blues arose.

In 1910, 80 per cent of all black people in the South lived in rural areas, and the explosion of black music and creativity reflected this demographic. To say that life was hard for southern blacks would be a gross understatement. Only a few decades on from the Civil War, the institutionalized racism that defined the south was still in full force. With separate facilities for blacks and whites, Jim Crow laws, weekly lynchings, and shifting seasonal employment, life for Southern Blacks was bleak but filled with promises of freedom and opportunity that were never delivered.

Many blacks were 'sharecroppers' and were little better off as free men than they were under slavery. Under the state laws of the 1890s, black farmhands were virtually prevented from leaving the land. If they were allowed to leave it was usually under the strict law of unscrupulous landowners. A one-time black sharecropper writing of his experience said, "Like other Negro sharecroppers, we were always moving, always in hope of finding a landlord who would not take advantage of us. But we hardly ever succeeded in bettering our position."

Jin Crow laws, ordering segregation in public places, spread throughout the area from 1890 to 1910, requiring separate accommodation for blacks and whites on railroads and other public areas. White supremacy and hatred of blacks increased as competition for jobs replaced the paternalism of slavery. The political and economic machinery favored whites and the frustrations of the freed slaves grew.

The church became the outlet for the blacks' frustrations; it was at this time that blues and gospel music began to evolve on parallel lines. Many early bluesmen were also preachers, e.g. Reverend Gary Davis and Son House. The church, however, often proved inadequate as an outlet, especially for young blacks, who were forced to move in order to find work.

It was both hard to leave and hard to stay for blacks in the South. Naturally, they had family ties and close relationships and these proved to be the only stabilizing factor in their lives. Yet, the world as it was defined for them was narrow and limiting, bound by fear and frustration. Often the hope of a better life was sought in the North, in cities like Chicago.

In the evolution of the music of the blues we can hear the culmination of these fears, frustrations, joys, sorrows, and longings. The bluesman Henry Townsend says, explaining the relevance of the blues to his audience, "People in general they takes the song as an explanation for themselves – they believe this song is expressing their feelings instead of the one that's singin' it." The blues becomes an escape for the people who are feeling frustrations and fears but are unable to express them. Perhaps this describes why blues is appreciated on a universal level, why not only blacks but people from other cultural backgrounds appreciate the blues, relating to the musical and emotional components in this music of frustration and longing. Regardless of race, nation, or sex, the blues connects people with the emotional urgency of hopes and desires that can never be fully met.

These were the conditions under which the blues tradition arose. But why don't the songs, in their lyrics, speak of the oppression? The music rarely discussed the roots of oppression, because to have done so would have opened the door to even more lynchings and hardship. Instead, the lyrical content of blues favored a general rather than specific dissatisfaction with life. It was, for instance, permissible to discuss the dissatisfactions in male-female relationships.

There were also stories of folk heroes such as John Henry and Stag-o-lee. These stories were usually warnings of what might happen to the 'bad man,' or what might happen if you stepped out of line. The lawman was always there to keep you in line. The lyrics were really a thinly-veiled metaphor for the oppression blacks felt.

The popularity of blues in the Mississippi Delta was particularly strong. The area's huge plantations were worked by sharecroppers. Blacks were also able to find work in a number of other occupations: building levees to hold back the waters of the 'Mighty' Mississippi, cutting timber, and building the railroads that would carry the crops to market. Where the work was hard – in mining towns, tobacco plantations, work camps, and prisons – the blues thrived in gambling dens, saloons, and brothels as well as in 'legitimate' house parties, fish fries, barbecue stands, and railway stations.

Around 1905, bandleader W.C. Handy was dozing at a train station in Tutwiler, Mississippi, when he had his first encounter with the blues. A young man approached him playing guitar and using a knife as a slide. Handy wrote about his encounter, "His clothes were rags; his feet peeped out of shoes. His face had on it some of the sadness of the ages… The singer repeated the line three times, accompanying himself on the guitar with the weirdest music I had ever heard. The tune stayed in my mind." For bandleaders like Handy and the general populace, the music of the era was saturated with novelty tunes and peppy numbers that would be forgotten in a week's time, like any number of Brittney

Spears songs. The music this young ragged man was playing "stayed" with Handy. Even though it was "weird" there was a quality that haunted him.

The lyrical qualities of blues could range from poetic to frank discussions of sex, to wails, moans and humming. The vocal was not merely an expression of words with musical notes attached. The vocal was delivered in the manner that was truthful to the expression of the artist. The non-lyrical quality of many of these performances is also wrapped up in the anguish that was the black experience. The guitar playing reflected this sentiment: it was a mournful wailing. It could be hard and visceral, or soft and playful. The slide guitarist could bring these sentiments to the fore with his voice, his guitar and his slide.

The music of the blues

But blues did not just show up on the doorstep one day; nor was it really 'discovered' by explorers like Handy. To say that any form of music was created in a vacuum would be wrong. This is especially true of rural American music, which was passed on from group to group and evolved through the contributions of both blacks and whites, as well as other races and cultures. In particular, blacks had adopted Anglo-American folk-ballads traditions and adapted them to their own musical traditions. Characters such as John Henry, a spike driver on a railroad who "died with a hammer in his hand," were created out of this folk-ballad tradition. Other folk characters, such as Stag-o-lee, were often 'bad men' who suffered for their transgressions: a black southern version of a morality play.

The white folk ballads were sung unaccompanied, but the black ballads incorporated the guitar, banjo, harmonica, and other instruments. Somewhere along the line the 'blue note' became a part of the blues vernacular. In musical terms the blue note is represented by a dynamic tension between two notes (most often the major and minor third, but sometimes including other notes of pentatonic and seven-note western scales, as well). The blues player would bend or slide back and forth between the two notes, sometimes resolving the tension and sometimes not. The blue note(s) has become as synonymous with the blues as the 12-bar structure.

(The 12-bar structure actually evolved later on with electric and ensemble blues. The solo artists of the earlier 20th century had a little more freedom with their interpretation of rhythmic structures. Sometimes they used 13 bars or 14, sometimes partial bars were included, and time signature shifts often occurred. It was all up to the individual to express the song in whatever rhythmic, melodic or non-melodic way they felt.)

Slide guitar helped emphasize the blue note by allowing the player to achieve that 'slippery' quality – that elusiveness that is integral to the blues. The blues, thought by many to be a technically limiting genre, has some deep nuances that are often difficult to explain. Musical phrasings are often individual interpretations: how different artists interpret the blue note(s) could be a subject for a long essay.

In the beginning no one considered himself strictly a blues musician. Indeed, the genre at this point had hardly been defined. Most of the players drew upon spirituals, ragtime tunes and other popular tunes of the day to perform in public. But the popularity of the music grew and bandleaders like W.C. Handy started to incorporate blues into their bands' sets. In the 1920s the phonograph replaced sheet music as the best way to promote the blues. This was a blessing and a curse in that now a larger audience was being exposed to the music via LPs: long playing records. Blues performers were beginning to make names for themselves. But their recordings were marketed as 'race' records and sold strictly to black audiences. Many of these records went virtually unnoticed until the advent of a more democratic radio system in the 1950s.

The first blues singers to record, in the early 1920s, were based in New York. They included Ma Rainey and Bessie Smith and were backed by the top jazz musicians of the day, including Louis Armstrong, King Oliver and Jelly Roll Morton.

In 1925 recording techniques improved and portability became a factor in transporting the equipment to the rural south. Electricity and the microphone were better suited to picking up the rural accents and guitar than the old acoustic horn technique. Record companies started sending people out to capture the sounds of rural America with the new portable recording equipment. These early sessions were held in rented motel rooms, churches and auditoriums.

THE RISE OF THE GUITAR:
Many factors led to the rise of the guitar as the featured instrument in blues. First, but not foremost, was the expansion of the railroad. Between 1860 and 1910, railroad construction averaged 4,000 miles per year. In the south the main construction linking it with the rest of the nation occurred between 1893 and 1904. With the railroad network firmly in place, postal delivery increased and thus was born the Sears and Roebuck catalog.

Ordering through a catalog, rural dwellers had access to goods that they had previously only dreamed of. Initially, the catalog didn't advertise musical instruments, but by 1905 more than 60 pages were dedicated to guitars, ukuleles, saxophones, trumpets, banjos, and violins.

Blacks, most likely, were not the initial purchasers of these instruments. In the 1897 catalog, guitars ranged in price from $3.25-$27.00, more than most blacks of the time could afford. As the novelty of the original purchase wore off, however, and the purchaser realized that playing the instrument required some work, the instruments often found their way to pawnshops. Blacks were often the fortunate beneficiaries of bored whites when it came to guitar pawnshop purchases.

Another factor in the rise of the guitar among bluesmen was the decline of the banjo. The banjo had been the main instrument of minstrel shows. The parodying of blacks in these shows had become less tolerable to the black community in a time of social change. However, many of the techniques that were used with banjos, such as open tunings, were transferred to the guitar. This was a major attraction for the slide player who used the open tunings to great advantage. Able to accompany themselves using finger-picking techniques like banjo players, the more skilled players could keep separate bass and melody lines going at the same time. Also the timbre of the guitar was better suited to the soloist's vocal register: the banjo having a raspier sound, and the guitar a mellower and more lyrical quality.

A host of blues pioneers sprang forth in this era of expansion. Many of the players had a style that could be associated with a particular area of the south. There was the Texas sound, the Delta sound and the Piedmont sound, to name a few. None had quite the impact of the early Delta players, who pioneered a style of playing that drifted northward to Chicago where it evolved into the electric blues we know today.

The evolution of the guitar

Guitars prior to the 1930s were small. As the demand for bass increased, the instrument became bigger. The dreadnought – named after a famous British battleship – was introduced by Martin in 1931. This became the favored instrument of country and Bluegrass pickers: with its boomy sound, guitarists could create a big sound with the emphasis on the bottom. Blues players, however, concentrated on licks and melodies and preferred the smaller-bodied Gibsons. Also, for financial reasons, blues artists favored the less expensive Stellas and Regals of the day.

Guitar necks, up until 1930, joined the body at the 12th fret. After 1930 it became fashionable to make guitars with necks that joined at the 14th fret, giving players access to higher notes. A lot of slide playing is centered around the 12th fret (especially in open tunings). Having access to higher frets could give the music that extra little nudge of wildness that would open the door to the slide playing histrionics of rock players

Resophonic Guitars

In 1927 when resophonic guitars first appeared on the market they were valued for their volume. Today, they are valued for their tone. In a normal wood guitar the vibration of the strings sets the whole top of the guitar in motion; with a resonator guitar the string vibration passes through the cone, a structure looking a little like a pie plate. Just like a loudspeaker, the cone of the resonator guitar amplifies the sound. Being made of metal, it gives the sound a metal twang. In order for the cone to amplify most effectively, resophonic guitars are usually strung with medium to heavy gauged strings and are played with finger picks.

These guitars seemed to have been designed with slide players in mind – although they weren't. There are not many sounds as distinctive as a slide being used on a resonator guitar. It spells rural blues. Particularly good for slide playing is the National Resonator guitar.

National was the company that introduced the resonator concept. Originally designed for the guitarist competing with saxophones, trumpets, drums and other instruments in an orchestra, it fell out of favor when electric guitars were introduced. However, Hawaiian and blues players seemed to capture the essence of the instrument with their slide techniques.

 The first design was the popular Tricone, comprised of three small resonators linked by a T-bar. The Tricone was by far the most sophisticated of the resonator instruments. These first instruments were made of brass with a nickel plating. They often had very ornate engravings: palm trees and Hawaiian Island themes predominated. In order to provide more economical versions of the resonator guitar the company introduced the single cone, Style O, and later the modestly priced Duolian. These later and more economical versions substituted steel for brass and had a harsher tone that was ideal for the tough sounds coming from artists such as Son House.

A few years after the first Nationals made their way to the market a split in the company led the Dopyera brothers (the original designers) to leave and start their own company: Dobro. Because of patent licenses, the Dopyeras were forced to design a new resonator style and hence the Dobro was born. In a dobro the cone is connected to the bridge indirectly via a strutwork apparatus called a 'spider' rather than the National T-bar and 'biscuit' bridges.

The different designs of cones lend different tonal qualities to Dobros and Nationals. Dobros tend to have a slightly 'nasal' quality. In Dobros the resonator is normally resting in a wood-topped guitar – in Nationals it is usually resting inside a metal guitar, although both companies made wood and metal models. Dobros tend to be favored by country and bluegrass musicians, and Nationals tend to be favored by blues musicians.

In the 1980s the National Guitar Company returned to making high-quality resonator instruments. The earlier models from the late 1920s and 1930s are still highly sought after, however, the new models are of a superior quality and sit high above most of the other resonator guitars on the market today.

PLAYERS:

Charlie Patton

Not enough can be said about the influence of Charlie Patton, who was born in 1891 near Bolton in Southern Mississippi. Some call Patton the original founder of the Delta blues – he was one of Robert Johnson's 'mentors.' Son House, Howlin' Wolf, Muddy Waters, Elmore James, and John Lee Hooker can all trace their styles back to Patton.

He was born in the late 1880s and lived on Will Dockery's plantation between Drew and Boyle in rural Mississippi. Patton began to have some success as a musician as early as 1910 but it wasn't until the late 1920s that he became recognized as 'the man.' Between 1929 and 1930 Patton recorded 42 issued sides, more than any other blues artist had turned out in one year. Patton's vocal style was steeped in a rich baritone; a voice that was both raw and visceral. His playing style was also raw and visceral; a great performer, Patton sometimes played the guitar behind his back or on his knees. He had a reputation as a drunk and as a womanizer (he reportedly had eight wives), and his hard living ended his life prematurely in 1934 at the age of 42.

He was a regional success and inspired many of the guitarists of the day, not only with his guitar playing and acrobatic performance style, but with his nice clothes, cars, fancy guitars, and female admirers.

He was a small, slight man with wavy hair who had inherited his mother's facial features: mixed Indian, black and white. His parents provided a stable atmosphere on their farm in Mississippi, hoping that Charlie would maintain their position in the community. Charlie, however, wanted to play guitar and have fun. When the family moved to the Dockery plantation, Patton started to learn guitar from a man named Henry Sloan.

In 1929 Patton met Henry Spier, a white music-store owner (and talent scout) who sent him north to record for the Paramount Blues label. His recordings represented him at his best and it was said that he was a much better singer on record than he was in live performance. However, the recordings didn't change his life much; he still had to perform every night to make a living. He continued to play for audiences all over the South, not just blacks but whites, as well.

He developed a couple of different slide techniques. Using both the knife blade and bottleneck techniques, Patton was able to get various effects from the guitar, creating high pitches by playing far up the fretboard; as well, he was able to use the sustaining quality of the slide for slow drag tunes, such as 'Banty Rooster.' In 'Mississippi Boweavil Blues' and 'Spoonful Blues' one can hear Patton's percussive alternating bass combined with flawless bottleneck technique.

Songs: 'Spoonful Blues,' 'Mississippi Boweavil Blues'

Guitar: Early Gibson or Stella

Son House

One of Patton's protégés was Son House. Son House (1902-1988) was not as well known as some of his peers, such as Robert Johnson and Charlie Patton, but he was one of the most powerful of the group. His playing was primitive, not flashy, and his vocal delivery was nothing if not impassioned. In his slide playing one could hear personal demons being fought, like the licking of flames at the boots of a mortal sinner.

Born near Lyon, Mississippi, House chopped cotton as a teenager while developing a passion for the Baptist church. At an early age he became a preacher but had a falling out with the church after having an affair with a woman ten years his senior.

In 1926 he began playing guitar, learning from an obscure local musician named James McCoy. But in 1928, at a house party near Lyon, House shot and killed a man. He was sentenced to work at Parchman Farm, a State penitentiary that also housed Bukka White, and that became notorious for its ill-treatment of its prisoners. A judge reexamined the case and House was released after 18 months. House was advised to leave the area and so he picked up and moved to the Clarksdale vicinity, where he struck up a friendship with Charlie Patton.

In 1930 House traveled with Patton to Grafton, Wisconsin, where he recorded his first sides. These early recordings established him as a powerful voice in the world of the blues. However, they did not lead to commercial success. There were no further recordings until Alan Lomax recorded him for the Library of Congress in 1941, and then again no recordings until the folk revival of the 1960s.

In the 1960s he could be seen at many festivals, playing his National resonator guitar and stomping his feet like a wild man. It was partly the rediscovery of House and his peers by a new white audience that helped propel a renewed interest in the blues. In his playing there was as much percussive attack – popping the strings, vocal groans – as there was melody. Often melody seemed to be sacrificed for the outpouring of emotion that came out in House's performances. He alternated his single note slide runs with descending bass lines. House truly seemed like a man haunted by demons. When he played slide it was like shards of glass on hard pavement, not always a pleasing sound, but a raw and truthful one.

Song: 'Empire State Blues'
Guitar: National Triolian, Duolian, or Style 0

Robert Johnson

The myth of Robert Johnson, the most influential of the early blues men, says that he sold his soul to the devil at the crossroads for his amazing guitar talent. He is credited with giving birth to rock'n'roll, and has influenced artists such as The Rolling Stones, Led Zeppelin, Eric Clapton and many others. Clapton plays tribute to Johnson on his 2004 recording, *Me and Mr. Johnson*, showcasing several songs from Johnson's repertoire. Today, if people are not familiar with who Johnson was, they certainly know his songs – 'Dust My Broom,' 'Sweet Home Chicago,' 'Walkin' Blues' – which have been repeatedly recorded by artists over the decades.

Robert Johnson was born May 8th, 1911, in Hazlehurst, Mississippi, to Julia Dodds and Noah Johnson. His ten siblings were fathered by another man, Charles Dodds. Apparently, Dodds was a furniture maker and landowner and financially solvent until a falling out with some local landowners. As the story goes, Dodds was being sought by a lynch mob and made his escape to Memphis by dressing like a woman.

Eventually, Julia Dodds was forced off her land for non-payment of taxes and spent the next eight years trying to reunite her children with their father, Charles. Robert was considered illegitimate and while he was eventually accepted by Charles Dodds, Dodds never accepted Julia back. Robert is said to have adopted the name of Johnson in his teens when he learned who his real father was. Perhaps some of the mystery revolving around Robert Johnson stems from the various monikers he adopted at different points in his life. He went by the names of Robert Spencer, R.L. Spencer, and sometimes Robert Dodds.

In 1914 Johnson went to live in Memphis with his adopted father and a family that included Dodds' children, mistress and their two children. It was here that Robert began to learn guitar from his brother, Charles Leroy.

Son House, speaking about Robert Johnson, says: "We'd play for Saturday night balls, and there would be this little boy hanging around. He blew a harmonica and he was pretty good with that, but he wanted to play guitar." The myth that Johnson sold his soul to the devil stems from this period. At the time that House was speaking of, Johnson couldn't play the guitar at all. When he next saw Johnson a few months later, guitar strung over his back, he was awed by Johnson's playing. It was thought that the boy had to have sold his soul to devil in order to get that good that quickly.

Not only had Johnson become proficient on the instrument, he was a gifted entertainer who established an immediate rapport with his audience. Wherever he went he was remembered for his warmth. His repertoire included not just the blues sides we have today, but whatever his audience wanted to hear: Bing Crosby tunes, country tunes, hillbilly tunes, Duke Ellington songs. His traveling companion, Johnny Shines, claims that Robert had an ability to play anything. He would hear it once and play it right back.

By the middle 1930s Robert was well known throughout the Delta areas and had followings in southern Mississippi and eastern Tennessee. He had wanted to make records for some years, as his mentors Willie Brown, Son House, and Charlie Patton had done. In 1936 Johnson got his chance to record, indirectly, through the same man who had recorded Son House, Patton, and Skip James. H.C. Spier was a white man working for ARC records and had recorded 200 sides in Jackson and Hattiesberg. Only 40 had been issued, however, so he passed Johnson's name on to Ernie Oertle, a talent scout and salesman for ARC in the mid-south. In November they traveled to San Antonio, TX. He recorded 16 sides in three days, including 'I Believe I'll Dust My Broom' and 'Kind Hearted Woman.'

In all, Johnson recorded 29 sides between 1936 and 1938, all of which have been reissued numerous times. He died in 1938 from poisoning by a jealous husband; he was 27 years old. Of his slide playing, probably his most memorable track is 'Come On In My Kitchen.' Johnson blended rhythm, lead, riffs, and vocals in a way that was entirely his own. He would play a slide line and moan along with it; he would then break into a shuffle rhythm and complement that with single-note lead lines.

All we have left to remember Johnson are those 29 sides and one photo in which he is wearing a fancy suit and holding a nice Gibson guitar (probably borrowed). His blues have a brooding sense of torment and despair. The mystery of what tormented Johnson is almost as provocative as his actual playing. In Peter Guralnick's book *Searching for Robert Johnson* it is easy to understand the appeal:

> "What could be more appropriate to our sense of romantic mystery than an emotionally disturbed poet scarcely able to contain his 'brooding sense of torment and despair'? ... So Robert Johnson became the personification of the existential blues singer, unencumbered by corporeality or history, a fiercely incandescent spirit who had escaped the bonds of tradition by the sheer thrust of genius."

For all the emotional impact the recordings of Robert Johnson left us, there is also this: he played some amazing guitar. His slide playing is of the highest caliber: he would use single line runs, and yet there was the multi-string triplet attack that powered tunes like 'Dust My Broom.' 'Come On In My Kitchen' has one of most recognizable and eloquent single string opening phrases ever recorded. That opening phrase combined with the hummed part are at once suggestive, sad and beautiful; pleading and at the same time demanding. Even if you are not a Robert Johnson fan there is no denying the influence passed down to future generations of blues and slide players.

Songs: 'Come On In My Kitchen,' 'Dust My Broom'

Guitar: Gibson L1

Tampa Red:

Tampa Red or 'The Guitar Wizard' was the first big star from Chicago's blues scene. His real name was Hudson Whittaker. Born in Smithsville Georgia, he was orphaned at an early age and moved to Tampa, Florida to live with his grandparents. The Red-headed Tampa worked as a musician on the vaudeville circuit until he moved to Chicago in the mid-1920s. In Chicago he started working with Tom Dorsey (not the orchestra leader) and together they invented a new kind of blues called hokum (light and peppy numbers filled with lyrical double-entendres).

Tampa played with the house band at Bluebird Records, helping to establish the 'Bluebird Beat,' which was the sound coming out of the Chicago record label at the time. He was also very helpful to those in the blues scene. He opened his house to other artists in need, fans, and foreign visitors.

Tampa continued to record into the early 1950s, but rock'n'roll was taking over most of the business. He retired in 1953, having recorded more than 320 sides. In 1955, his wife Frances died. Tampa struggled with this and began to drink heavily. In 1960, he cut two more albums for the Prestige-Bluesville label and completely retired. He died in a nursing home on March 19th, 1981, the same year he was inducted into the Blues Foundation's Hall of Fame.

Tampa Red was a huge influence on bottleneck players of the era. He often played with a band or accompanist, which allowed him to stretch out and play some complicated single-note slide runs. He also helped popularize National resonator guitars with the blues crowd. He was usually seen playing a National Tricone guitar, an instrument with a more sophisticated sound than its brother, the single-resonator (Style O and Duolian), played by Son House.

Song: 'Denver Blues'
Guitar: National Tricone

Mississippi Fred McDowell

Born in Rossville, Tennessee, in 1904, Fred McDowell eventually settled in Mississippi in 1940. In his younger days, McDowell played for tips on the streets of Memphis, but decided that life on the road wasn't for him and became a farmer. During the week he tended the farm and on the weekends he played house parties and fish fries.

He did not record until 1959 when folklorist Alan Lomax found him and recorded him for the American Folk Music series on Atlantic Records. In 1964, Chris Strachwitz of Arhoolie records hunted down McDowell and recorded a two volume series which helped propel him into the radar of the Folk revivalists.

During this period McDowell performed at coffee houses and the famous Newport Folk Festival. The Rolling Stones invited him to Europe to play. The Stones reportedly bought McDowell a silver lamé suit that he wore back home and was eventually buried in.

He first learned guitar from an uncle who used a hollowed-out bone for a slide. McDowell was by all accounts a gracious man who freely shared his knowledge of blues and the guitar. He even set up a foundation before he died, using money from his record sales to buy instruments for underprivileged children in Northern Mississippi.

Song: 'Goin' Down to the River'

Blind Boy Fuller

Some say that Blind Boy Fuller (also known as Fulton Allen) was to the Piedmont blues what Robert Johnson was to the Delta blues. The Piedmont is the area of the Southeast United States bordered by the coast and the mountain foothills. He was one of the best selling blues artists of the 1930s, and his songs were learned and covered by many of the East Coast bluesmen who followed. Perhaps he is not as well known as Johnson because Piedmont blues, with its emphasis on ragtime, had less of an influence on the Chicago blues (and rock'n'roll) than the Delta musicians. The hard-driving sounds of the Delta blues lent them a sophistication and flair that the more rural-sounding Piedmont blues lacked.

Fuller was born in 1907 or thereabouts in Wadesboro, North Carolina, southeast of Charlotte. He was one of the few members of his family who took an interest in music, and even he didn't begin to take it seriously until his early twenties. He married a woman named Cora, who became his wife at the tender age of 14. Shortly after their marriage, Fuller began having trouble with his eyesight and became increasing dependent on Cora for help. It was also about this time that he became more interested in music – blindness and being black severely limiting his employment options. Under the tutelage of The Reverend Gary Davis, Fuller gained first competence and then mastery of his chosen instrument, the guitar.

He was earning a decent living busking on the streets of Durham, NC, when he was noticed by J.B. Long, a white man who managed the United Dollar Store. Long had been drumming up country and gospel talent for the American Record Company, and in 1935 he convinced them to record Fuller. The sessions took place in New York with Gary Davis and Richard Trice brought on board. The recordings went so well that Fuller was asked back as a solo artist in April of 1936. Later collaborations included a stint with harmonica legend Sonny Terry.

In 1938 Fuller was diagnosed with arrested syphilis. His health continued to falter and he died on February 13th, 1941.

Guitar: National 12- and 14-fret Duolians
Song: 'Homesick And Lonesome Blues'


Robert Nighthawk

Robert Nighthawk was a drifter. He was born Robert McCullum on November 30th, 1909, in Helena, Arkansas. His travels brought him into contact with Charlie Patton, Robert Johnson, John Lee Hooker, Muddy Waters, Elmore James and B.B. King. In the mid 1930s he left the Deep South, where he was reported to have shot a man, for St. Louis. In the late 1930s he returned to Chicago to record 'Prowling Night-Hawk,' one of his most popular records. Thus, was Robert 'Nighthawk' created.

His slide playing is smooth, some would say 'liquid.' His single-string melodies complemented his dark and melancholy-tinted voice.

Black Ace

One of the few blues players to use a National Tricone square-neck played on his lap, Black Ace seems to have represented a crossover between blues and Hawaiian guitar. His playing is a bit more sophisticated than Robert Johnson's or Son House's, but he never acquired the same fame as those two. However, he is an important figure in the history and legacy of slide guitar.

In the late 1930s, a Texan by the name of Babe Karo Lemon Turner released a single called, 'Black Ace Blues.' A local radio station picked up on the name and it soon became the moniker by which the artist would be known. He disappeared until Chris Strachwitz came to his home in Fort Worth, Texas, in 1960 and recorded him for Arhoolie Records. Along with the earlier recordings from the 1930s, these are the only recordings that exist from Black Ace. Partly because of his lack of a prolific recording career and partly because his playing is not associated with any regional style (e.g. Piedmont, Chicago), Ace is a bit of an obscurity. However, in his playing one can hear the blend of a gracious melodic sense, more associated with Hawaiian music, and a blues rhythmic structure.

Song: 'Black Ace Blues'

Guitar: National Tricone

## THE BLUES MOVES NORTH

## CHICAGO

In the 1940s, as blacks left the South for work in the factories up North, the blues also left. Chicago became the cultural center for blues and was the city that launched the careers of artists such as Muddy Waters, Big Bill Broonzy, Tampa Red and others looking for recording opportunities. When the music moved to this new urban location it began to transform from its rural roots to a more modern sound. Acoustic guitar players began favoring the new electric guitar, and combos were formed to compete with the volume of rent parties. The new sound had an excitement that was partly inspired by the jump-blues combos of the late 1940s. These bands used swing rhythms, honking saxophones and racy lyrics to pepper their set and keep the people smiling and dancing.

Big Bill Broonzy, who had been relatively successful as a solo artist, incorporated a combination of piano, second guitar, horns and drums into his sound. Muddy Waters used the electric guitar for great effect, launching angry and aggressive slide runs. Waters had started out as a solo acoustic musician, but when he played electric with a band it transformed the music from its lonely rural southern roots to a lively urban sound that electrified the dance floors and virtually paved the way for rock'n'roll. His recordings inspired many of the British rock legends of the sixties to play blues and seek out old recordings.

Muddy Waters

McKinley Morganfield was born in 1915, in Rolling Rock, Mississippi. He garnered the name 'Muddy' because he loved to play in the water of nearby Deer Creek. At age seven he fell in love with the harmonica. His family attached 'Waters' to the nickname, and it stuck.

His rich tenor voice, singing slightly behind the beat, and a style of slide playing that emphasized the bass strings – as opposed to most slide players who played leads runs on the treble strings – produced a distinctive voice in the blues.

He recorded for the famous Library of Congress musicologist, Alan Lomax, in 1941. After hearing the recordings he became convinced of his own commercial viability. He moved to Chicago in 1943 where he found work playing rent parties. He gained commercial success with the 1947 release *I Can't be Satisfied*, which quickly sold out several pressings. He returned to the Deep South and often toured there throughout the

1950s and 1960s with John Lee Hooker. In 1958 he toured England and opened the door for bluesmen from the US to play in the UK.

Muddy Waters became a more direct influence on future musicians. He brought the solo rural blues and wedded it to a small ensemble, thus defining Chicago's electric blues sound. When the "hoochie-coochie man" got his "mojo workin'" he was a hard man to beat. Muddy Waters died April 30th, 1983, and is buried in Chicago.

Waters was one of the first to amplify his guitar. In increasingly loud venues it became necessary to bring up the volume; as he did so, the guitar had a tendency to distort. This distortion begins to compress the guitar signal, producing increased sustain. The combination of increased distortion and sustain opened a new world for slide guitarists: the sound evolved and players such as Elmore James, Duane Allman, Rory Gallagher and Rod Price used it to create a new sound palette on which slide guitarists could paint their effervescent landscapes.

As the sound evolved, the guitar was able to emulate not only the human voice but other instruments as well. Heretofore, the natural decay of the sound was rather quick. But with the sustain of electric guitar, the glissando could travel over the interval of several notes: the guitarist could pick one note, for example, and with the use of the slide land on 4 or 5 more notes before even needing to pick again. Like a horn player, who was only limited by the amount of wind he could muster, the guitar player could slide more freely between notes. Certain overtones were created; notes between notes became more useful and interesting.

Song: 'Hoochie Coochie Man'
Guitar: Fender Telecaster

Elmore James
Along with Muddy Waters, Elmore James is one of the few players represented in this book who bridges the gap between the old delta blues players and the modern blues and rock'n'roll players. He is classified as a post-war musician, not having made his first recordings until 1951. However, he did quite a lot of playing between 1929-50, having shared the stage with such luminaries as Robert Johnson and Sonny Boy Williamson II.

He was born Elmore Brooks in 1918 in Richland, Mississippi. His family moved up and down Highway 51, going from plantation to plantation in search of work. At the age of ten he was playing a self-made guitar, as well as other 'home-made' instruments such as the 'diddley bow.' Over the next ten years he refined his playing on the streets, at fish fries and jook joints. In 1937 the family moved to Belzoni. James's parents adopted another child, Robert Earl Holsten, and the two young men began to play music together in Belzoni. The same year, at age 19, James married a young woman named Josephine Harris. James, however, seemed restless and the wandering life of the road called. This was also the year that James met two very important men: Robert Johnson and harmonica player, Alec 'Rice' Miller. Johnson's bottleneck playing left a deep impression on James and it was a style he would emulate and become famous for. He began to travel more often and met Sonny Boy Williamson, who was beginning to make a name for himself from his short performance on radio station KFFA's new show advertising King Biscuit Flour (the radio show grew in popularity over the years and had the largest audience in the south for blues in the following decades).

In 1943 he was inducted into the Navy, taking part in the invasion of Guam. By 1945 he was back home in Belzoni, sharing a room with Sonny Boy Williamson. In the early 1940s he began playing electric guitar, using distortion and sustain to create a dense sound.

James's first recording for the Trumpet label was Robert Johnson's 'Dust my Broom' which went to number nine on the national R & B charts. The following year he relocated to Chicago, where he recorded with numerous record companies, including Modern, Chess, Chief, Fire, Fury and Enjoy Records. He continued to record and perform throughout the 1950s and 1960s. James died on May 24th, 1963, in Chicago, at the age of 45.

Elmore James brought the sound of the Delta to the modern world. He was employing the techniques of Robert Johnson and Charlie Patton, but with an electric guitar and a backing band. This gave the music an energy that propelled it into the sphere of rock'n'roll. You could also say that James helped the world recognize the connection between blues and Hawaiian music – he even recorded a song called 'Hawaiian Boogie.' He left a legacy of slow blues, boogies and rave ups that inspired such modern day guitarists as Johnny Winter, Rod Price and Rory Gallagher, to name but a few.

Song: 'Dust My Broom'

DETROIT

Detroit also became a center for electric blues, launching the careers of such notables as John Lee Hooker. His 'Boogie Chillen' was an extremely popular post-war blues record and placed him on a level with Waters as one of the most popular blues musicians of the time. 'Boogie Chillen,' a danceable boogie that was dark and spooky, harkened to darker themes in the underbelly of blues. Much of Hooker's influence can be heard in the playing of Billy Gibbons of ZZ Top.

NEW YORK

Many of the bluesmen who wound up in New York were from Virginia, the Carolinas and Georgia. The blues in this part of the country were ragtime influenced, with lots of finger-picking. Players such as the Reverend Gary Davis, Sonny Terry and Brownie McGee, and Mississippi John Hurt played their rural blues intact and were embraced by Folk revivalists such as Pete Seeger and Bob Dylan.

After his release from prison in 1934, Leadbelly (also known as Huddie Ledbetter), moved to New York and went to work for the Lomax family (chroniclers of American folk music for the Library of Congress), and fell in with Woody Guthrie and Pete Seeger.

The stylistic evolution of the blues ended in the 1960s as the civil rights movement began to take hold. Many of the victories of civil rights ameliorated many of the social factors that had contributed to the rise of the blues as a form of expression. The civil rights movement stressed collective action and had little use for the individualistic stance of the blues artist. At the same time, however, interest in the blues began to increase among whites, especially those involved in the folk revival.

THE FOLK REVIVAL

Folk music is a general term for roots music that has been handed down from generation to generation via participation in groups or person to person. The folk music revival of the 1950s and 1960s actively sought out the music of America's past: blues, country, Appalacian. This was music that had been created before the advent of recording technology; it is 'the music of the land.' Many of the people seeking and documenting it were people who weren't actually involved in creating it, namely, young white educated people.

Although much criticism has been aimed at the revivalists, a good argument exists for their promotion of the music: imitating the art of another culture gives that culture acknowledgement and visibility. If it weren't for the revivalists, many of the old blues artists might have been completely forgotten and acoustic slide guitar could have been totally lost:

> "The movement values above all else the intimacy of personal expression, created by soloists and small ensembles; though the folk revival sometimes mobilized large crowds, its soul was found in intimate gatherings and informal sing-alongs. The roots music that the revival emulated seems to stand for the same kind of personal interactions."

From 'The Flowering Of The Folk Revival,' by Alan Jabbour, in *American Roots Music*, edited by Robert Santelli, Holly George-Warren, and Jim Brown.

One path these revivalists took was to try and duplicate not so much the songs of the past, but the sound. They modeled their voices on the hillbilly musicians they loved, but put their own stamp on the music by writing their own lyrics and expanding the structure through jamming and instrumental experimentation. Guitarists recaptured the techniques of the early blues artists and sought out vintage instruments to make the sounds they had heard on early 78s by Robert Johnson, Son House, and Charlie Patton, such as old Gibsons, Nationals and Dobros. In 1952 the pioneering work of Harry Smith was revealed in the six LP *Anthology of American Folk Music*, a collection of blues, hillbilly and other folk music from the 1920s. Even today, this anthology stands out as the primer for anyone wishing to indoctrinate himself in American roots music. The *Anthology* was the working bible of the revivalists.

PLAYERS

John Fahey

One of these educated youngsters was a man named John Fahey. Fahey, with a background in philosophy at the University of California in Berkeley, was one of a handful of young white men who brought the senior bluesmen out of the woodwork. Son House, Skip James, Gary Davis, and John Hurt were able to enjoy a second artistic life in their old age, thanks in part to men like Fahey.

Fahey absorbed their music like a sponge. In the process he brought influences as eclectic as classical music and Indian ragas. His acoustic instrumentals combine the haunting qualities of early blues with the structural development of classical compositions and a droning quality reminiscent of Indian music. His slide playing reflected the stark quality of players like Charlie Patton and Black Ace.

The eccentric and idiosyncratic Fahey was raised in Takoma Park, Maryland. Born in 1939, the son of a US public health service employee, Fahey had an unhappy childhood and turned to the radio for solace. In 1954 he heard Bill Monroe's version of Jimmie Rodgers' 'Blue Yodel No.7,' which he claims changed his life forever. Another formative tune was Blind Willie Johnson's 'Praise God I'm Satisfied,' a song which made him weep.

Fahey went on to graduate studies in folklore and mythology at the University of California in Los Angeles — his Masters thesis was an exploration of the music and life of Charlie Patton. As part of his 'research,' Fahey tracked down the 'missing' blues artists

Bukka White and Skip James. Skip James, at the time, had lost interest in music but was tired of work as a tenant farmer. So in 1964 he joined in with the folk revivalists and revived his own career.

In 1959 Fahey recorded his first album, with money he had earned from pumping gas. He made 95 copies. One side of the plain white wrapper said 'John Fahey', and the other said 'Blind Joe Death,' an invented blues artist about whom Fahey made up an entire mythology.

Fahey then started Takoma Records, whose artists included the young Leo Kottke and Peter Lang. It almost seemed that starting his own company was necessary, since his eccentricities led him to assimilate such diverse sources as classical, Indian ragas, blues and bluegrasss – an unlikely mix that a record company would have a hard time labeling, let alone promoting. Somehow, all these influences mixed into a musical stew that left the listener engaged if not totally changed by the experience.

Fahey called his style of guitar 'American Primitive.' Guitarist and guitar teacher Les Weller describes the style:

> "American Primitive Guitar is grounded in our complex melting-pot American musical traditions. Hymns, rags, folk songs, jazz, classical, opera, eastern rhythms, contemporary tunes, and a galaxy of other musical sources contribute to this diverse form. Technique is based on using the multiple strings of the guitar to present the melody or theme supported by harmony and bass tones played simultaneously. Alternating bass is a regular feature, used in many forms to create a syncopation to support or contrast with other elements of the pieces. Varied tunings of the guitar enhance the instrument's tone, the playing of open strings reinforcing root tones and making multi-string techniques more accessible."

Fahey's eccentricities gave him an aura of mystery; and his penchant for drinking onstage gave his performances a certain unpredictability. He was said to have turned his back on his audience from time to time while performing on stage. It is said that his record sales actually went down after public appearances.

An American original, Fahey lived his life like he played his music. He disappeared from public performances, survived three divorces, wound up homeless and in the end died from complications from heart surgery. Still, he paved the way for artists such as Leo Kottke and Peter Finger and started a renaissance for acoustic guitar playing.

Song: 'Steel Guitar Rag'
Guitars: various Gibson acoustics, Bacon and Day.

Leo Kottke

The 1969 release of Leo Kottke's *6- and 12-String Guitar* came like a breath of fresh air for acoustic guitar fanatics who loved the sound of acoustic guitar but didn't care for the jangly associations of the post-folk-hippie revival. It was as if Leo had swallowed a bunch of old blues albums and a bottle of amphetamines at the same time. The music on that album seemed to set out to make a point: let's infuse acoustic guitar with the energy of rock'n'roll but keep the rural sensibilities of early blues. Listening to the album for the first time is like going for a hayride. Leo's adrenaline-infused guitar instrumentals, combined with his onstage dry wit and beautiful renditions of compositions such as Bach's 'Jesu, Joy of Man's Desiring' made him the biggest success in the world of acoustic guitar virtuosos. Many a college dorm in 1969 was filled with the stale smoke of marijuana and young men scratching their heads saying, "How'd he do that?"

Early in his career Kottke aligned himself with John Fahey's Tacoma label. The two seemed like a compatible duo, yet there are marked differences in their approaches. Kottke is more accessible and 'amped-up,' whereas Fahey is more moody, slower, and wistful. Both are wonderful slide players. On Kottke's 'Vaseline Machine Gun' he establishes a driving, almost relentless groove based on the lower strings, then breaks in to a slide phrase combined with an alternating bass that keeps the stew cooking. 'Watermelon,' another testosterone-driven tune, has such an uplifting feel you would have a hard time sitting down.

Kottke forgoes single string runs in favor of working his slide-playing around a solid bass-driven groove.

Nobody outside of Leadbelly has done as much to further the popularity of the 12-string guitar. Kottke made his name by exploring the tonalities of this instrument and if you have never played slide on a 12 string it is a real treat. The key is to use medium to heavy gauge strings and tune the guitar down. Kottke often tunes his guitar two to three half steps down. This will increase the 'growl factor' of your guitar and is essential for recreating the chunky sound as opposed to the more airy sound of the standard folk-oriented 12-string guitar.

Later recordings by Kottke tend to have a little less 'starch' but are well worthwhile even though he seems to have left the slide behind.

Song: 'Vaseline Machine Gun'
Guitars: Taylor 6- and 12-string

ROCK'N'ROLL

Rock'n'roll is essentially an amalgam of blues styles, including electric country blues, Kansas City blues, and Chicago and New Orleans blues. Chuck Berry and Bo Diddley introduced sounds from Chicago blues, while Fats Domino and Little Richard introduced elements of New Orleans blues. Rock pumped up the volume, speed and excitement of blues.

In rock'n'roll the electric guitar became king, president and prime minister. With its increased volume and sustain, as well as string-bending and distortion, the guitar could go places that it hadn't gone before. It became a more evocative instrument, duplicating the sound of the voice as well as horns and other instruments. Slide playing also evolved. With distortion came an infinite sustain that gave slide phrases a rawness and immediacy that the earlier acoustic bottleneck playing only hinted at.

Interestingly enough, a discussion of rock'n'roll, and specifically slide guitar in rock, harkens back to the ubiquitous Robert Johnson. In 1961 an album of Johnson's recordings (recorded in 1936 and 1937) was released with little fanfare. Nevertheless, Johnson became a minor pop star. During his lifetime only 12 songs had been released and none, except 'Terraplane Blues,' sold particularly well. But with the release of *King of the Delta Blues Singers* in 1961, a new generation was becoming cognizant of the blues man who had been cut off in his prime. On the cover of Bob Dylan's *Bringing It All Back Home* (1965) was a photo of miscellaneous bohemian 'stuff,' including *King of the Delta Blues Singers* featured prominently. Eric Clapton, all of 15 or 16 years old when the album came out, remembers, "I don't think I'd even heard of Robert Johnson when I found the record… It was a real shock that there was something that powerful. It all led me to believe that there was this guy who really didn't want to play for people at all, that this thing was so unbearable for him to have to live with that he was almost ashamed of it. This was an image I was very, very keen to hang on to."

Clapton's feelings, although very personal, struck a chord with the anti-establishment youth. In Johnson's singing and playing was an anguish; a search for fulfillment of desires so overpowering that to attain them seemed impossible. For the up and coming rockers, Johnson's playing and anguish were akin to their own feelings of dissatisfaction. Johnson's music was thrilling and fearful; just the recipe for people bored with the complacency of middle-class life.

For the young generation this was *new* music. It helped that there was the mythical aspect of Johnson's life and his 'mysterious' death. Was he really killed? How was he killed? Poisoned? Stabbed? Did he sell his soul to the devil, as bluesmen like Son House used to say to explain away his amazing talent? Johnson's raw emotionality lent itself to the young generation's disenfranchisement with the establishment. Robert Johnson dared to ask questions: What is a man's place in this world? Why is he cursed to want more than he can have?

Johnson was also relatively young when he recorded. He didn't have the wisdom and dignity of older bluesmen such as Son House and Skip James. In Johnson's recordings there is an element of shock that is lacking from the elder statesmen of blues.

There is also the musical complexity of Johnson's music, requiring more than one person could bring to it. Keith Richards recalls a visit to his art school pal, Brian Jones: "I'd just met Brian, and I went round to his apartment – crash pad, actually. All he had in it was a chair, a record player, and a few records, one of which was Robert Johnson. He put it on and it was astounding stuff… To me he was like a comet or a meteor that came along and BOOM, suddenly he raised the ante. Suddenly you just had to aim that much higher."


BRITISH BLUES

The British invasion of the 1960s helped Americans discover their own music. While America was feasting on Elvis, doo-wop bands and surf music, British youth were discovering the old bluesmen. Brian Jones, Keith Richards, Eric Clapton, Jimmy Page, Jeff Beck, George Harrison, and Peter Green could all trace their inspiration back to the blues.


Part of what helped inspire these musicians was the series of American Folk Blues Festivals held in Europe between 1962 and 1970. The impact of huge music festivals such as Woodstock, Monterey Pop, and The Newport Folk Festival is hard to deny. However, of equal, if not more, importance – for the British and indirectly the US as well – were the American Folk Blues Festivals. Here, young British musicians like Mick Jagger, Brian Jones, and Jimmy Page were given first-hand exposure to some of the leading early bluesmen. It must have been incredible to hear Lonnie Johnson playing an electric guitar in 1963, Mississippi Fred McDowell playing slide on electric, and John Lee Hooker, looking confident if not a little scary, strutting out an incredible version of 'Hobo Blues.'

There was a burgeoning blues scene in England, but it was small and had yet to fully establish itself. The sole English show in the first year of the festival, at the Manchester Free Trade Hall in 1962, was more of a word-of-mouth affair, but attracted the likes of Jagger and Richards. At the end it was all chaos, with people everywhere… The festival was originally designed to be a single tour, but was so successful it prompted future bookings.

The musicians were treated like royalty and the show, while being a bit staged, was a class act. "The first time I went to Europe was 1962," says John Lee Hooker, in his biography *Boogie Man,* "and boy it was just like the President or Jesus comin' in… Every night was a sellout. Standing room only, no matter how big the place was." The musicians dressed in suits and the stage was decorated with images of Delta towns and the rural South.

Blues in England began to hit the charts and more press was devoted to the blues. The fledgling publication *Blues Unlimited*, founded in 1963 was becoming increasingly popular, and *Melody Maker*, which previously had only covered jazz, began to devote more space to blues.

The festival brought acts like Lightnin' Hopkins, Howlin' Wolf, Willie Dixon and Sonny Boy Williamson onto the European Stage. The Rolling Stones even decided to cover Wolf's 'Little Red Rooster,' releasing it as their fifth UK single. The single, featuring Brian Jones's slide work, raced to number one on the charts and cemented the love affair England has had with American blues ever since.

The Yardbirds

Jimmy Page was an early innovator (and blues aficionado), and Jeff Beck continues to be an innovative voice in the world of guitar. But of all the guitar heroes produced by the 1960s group The Yardbirds, it is Eric Clapton who continually pays tributes to his blues roots. From his early days in John Mayall's Blues Breakers, covering Freddie King's 'Hideaway,' to his 2004 tribute to Robert Johnson, *Me and Mr Johnson*, Clapton has proven his mettle as a 21st century spokesman for the blues. He is not known as a slide player as such, but his collaborations with Allman Brothers guitarist Duane Allman helped bring to public awareness an incredible music talent. He has consistently brought blues musicians to the fore and made the rest of us take note of his influences.

Jimmy Page

A discussion of rock guitarists hardly seems appropriate without mentioning Jimmy Page. While Led Zeppelin innovated in the world of heavy metal and rock, they consistently drew on the early blues recordings for inspirations. Page was often dipping into the well of Robert Johnson and Elmore James riffs. His use of slide, however, was only one color in his sonic palette. One could say that Page's true genius was in the way he mixed sounds from all kinds of guitars and styles of playing (also, as producer of all the Led Zeppelin albums he is to be highly commended). Page could play boogie, Celtic finger-style, blues, jazz-infused flourishes. His early recordings helped define the intense distorted rock sound that would become synonymous with Heavy Metal.

His sound featured a Fender Telecaster and Vox AC30 amplifiers – moving on to the Les Paul and Marshall 100-watt stacks of later Zeppelin recordings. He blended acoustic guitar, open tunings, mandolin, theremin, and of course a violin bow across the string of an electric guitar.

Page began playing guitar at the age of 15. Along with his friend, Jeff Beck, he played in pickup bands around England. His poor health (bouts of fatigue) confined him to the studio, where he became an in-demand session player, appearing on albums by The Who, The Rolling Stones, Donovan, Joe Cocker and other popular British artists. The Yardbirds asked him to join, but instead he recommended Jeff Beck. Finally, in 1966 he did join the Yardbirds, but as their bassist. The union lasted two years and the band broke up. Page enlisted a friend from the session scene, bassist John Paul Jones, and teamed up with vocalist Robert Plant and Plant's drummer friend, John Bonham. This new band called itself *The New Yardbirds* (to fulfill contractual obligations) and toured Scandinavia. Upon return to England they had changed their name to Led Zeppelin (thanks to Keith Moon's comment that they would go over like a "lead balloon.")

The early Zeppelin albums, in particular, leaned on early blues for inspiration. Page also used some innovative tunings, including DADGAD ('Black Mountain Side,' 'Kashmir') and CACGCE ('Friends,' 'Bon-Yr-Aur').

Song: 'In My Time of Dying'
Guitar: Gibson Les Paul, Danelectro

Brian Jones

Known mainly as one of the founding guitarists of The Rolling Stones along with Keith Richards, Brian Jones was also a member of Britain's first all-white blues band: Blues Incorporated. While the constantly shifting ranks of the band included most of the original members of the Rolling Stones, it also included such luminaries as Ginger Baker and Jack Bruce. The Stones actually evolved out of this band and went on to incorporate more rockin' sounds into their mix. However, the blues sound continued to influence The Stones' writing. With other bands, such as The Yardbirds, Savoy Brown, and Ten Years After, they established a new genre: blues-rock.

In the early days, Jones held down the lion's share of The Stones' rhythm and slide playing, while Richards handled most of the lead work. Richards' Chuck Berry-influenced playing showed on covers of 'Route 66' and 'Carol,' while Jones' triplet-based licks sparked up Elmore James-style tunes like 'Little Red Rooster,' and 'I Wanna Be Your Man.'

Towards the end of the 1960s, Jones became less interested in the guitar and took up the sitar, dulcimer and marimba, leaving the bulk of guitar playing on Stones records to

Richards. In 1969 Jones he the Stones to pursue a solo career. A month later he drowned in his swimming pool.

If Keith Richards helped a new generation appreciate Chuck Berry, it was Jones who is owed thanks for helping introduce Elmore James and Robert Johnson to British blues devotees. He strayed from these roots – and in doing so he inspired some of the Stones more creative and experimental efforts – but the early recordings do firmly establish him as one of England's founding white blues musicians.

Song: 'Little Red Rooster'
Guitar: Vox teardrop

George Harrison

'My Sweet Lord' has some of the most wistful, memorable (and infinitely hummable) slide licks around. The slide work on The Beatles' 'Something' is beautiful; like most of Harrison's guitar work it is simple, unique and representative of the man's incredible talent. The 'quiet' Beatle was not only a tremendous guitarist but a great songwriter in his own right – even though Lennon/McCartney got most of the accolades.

The youngest Beatle, born in 1943, Harrison grew up in a strict household and had to sneak out of the house to play his first gig with his brother, Peter. Riding the bus to school with his friend, Paul McCartney, the two would often stop off at each others' houses to listen to records. George was too young at 14 to join Paul's group, The Quarrymen, but he hung out with the group and emulated his hero, John Lennon. Eventually, well, you know what happened… Ed Sullivan, screaming girls, *A Hard Day's Night*… Maharishi Mahesh Yogi… Eric Clapton steals his wife… *All Things Must Pass*…a brilliant solo career… Traveling Wilburys… an unsuccessful battle with cancer… We miss him dearly.

The spiritual center of The Beatles, Harrison was responsible for introducing the group to a varied palette of musical influences, just as Brian Jones had with The Rolling Stones. Those influences included the middle eastern sitar and, of course, slide guitar. Harrison's early influences were Carl Perkins and Andres Segovia. He worked hard to master a precise picking technique that would become useful in his sitar arrangements.

Harrison's playing was never big on histrionics. Instead he used subtle and catchy guitar lines. His lead playing always played to the song. Of course, the Beatles were never a jam band. Songwriting was brought to a level that has gone unsurpassed since the inception of the Fab Four. All musical expression was in the service of the song. Even with George Martin at the helm of The Beatles' recordings, it is the songs, melodies and lyrical content that we all remember.

Even as a solo artist, Harrison never went the route of other lead guitarists: putting his chops above his art. An understated player, he sought a higher ground, where all things would pass…

Songs: 'Something,' 'My Sweet Lord'
Guitar: Fender Stratocaster


Rod Price

One of my most vivid sonic memories of the 1970s is the sound of Foghat's 'Slowride' coming on the radio as we were headed down the road towards teenage oblivion. Rod Price's slide work on the track felt like it was coming apart at the seams, which was emblematic of our own lives. No other player comes to mind who represents the sheer wildness of rock slide playing like Price.

Price's first introduction to guitar was hearing Big Bill Broonzy on the radio. Then came Scrapper Blackwell, Elmore James, Robert Johnson and Muddy Waters, all of whom inspired Rod to play the blues-flavored music he loved.

His first band, Shakey Big City Blues Band, was heralded by Champion Jack Dupree as "the best blues band in Europe." One of his next projects was Black Cat Bones, where he replaced Paul Kossoff (founding guitarist of Free, the 1970s band). In Foghat, he was dubbed "the magician of slide." Three platinum and eight gold records later Rod has become a bona fide star.

Foghat was founded in 1971 by Price and 'Lonesome' Dave Peverett on vocals and second guitar, Roger Earl on drums and Tony Stevens on bass. The band cut its teeth on Chicago-based blues by artists like Willie Dixon, but its big hits came with originals: 'Fool For the City,' 'I Just Want to Make Love to You,' and the aforementioned 'Slow Ride.' Their music suffered somewhat from 1970s era bombast, but Price's slide playing is still worth listening to. They reached their height in 1977 with the release of *Foghat Live*, but in the 1980s they fell into obscurity. Various incarnations lasted until Peverett's death in 2000.

Price has carried on and has released several solo recordings. Over the years he has worked with John Lee Hooker, Muddy Waters and several other blues artists.

Song: 'Slow Ride'
Guitar: Gibson Les Paul

Rory Gallagher

Rory Gallagher is probably best known for producing straight-ahead blues-flavored rock. During the mid 1970s, when arena rock was in vogue and bands seem to favor performances and recordings of an epic nature, Gallagher's stripped-down format was a breath of fresh air. He played the most beat-up 1959 Stratocaster on the planet and his pension for wearing plaid shirts reinforced his image as the working man's guitarist. A fiery player who blended blues sensibilities with rock'n'roll excitement, Gallagher was a player first and a rock star second. Known for his friendly demeanor, he kept up a touring pace in the early 1970s that would have killed most people and nearly exhausted his band.

He first came to the attention of the world during the mid-1960s in a band called Taste. Taste, a power trio, blended American blues with the new sounds of heavy metal. The band broke up in 1971 and Gallagher went solo. He began to garner a big following in Europe and the United States. While Gallagher did not pioneer any particular sounds – unlike contemporaries such as Jimmy Page and Jeff Beck – he gave an excitement to blues-driven rock albums like *Against the Grain* and *Photo Finish*. His slide playing is reminiscent of Elmore James with a shot of adrenaline.

Song: 'Souped Up Ford'
Guitar: Stratocaster

MEANWHILE, BACK IN THE U.S…

Thanks, in part, to their British counterparts, Americans were rediscovering their own music: the blues.

Duane Allman

Duane Allman's short but explosive career would not only help define the roots of Southern rock, but his slide playing became the pinnacle to which guitar players then and now would aspire.

Born in Tennessee in 1946, Duane moved to Daytona Beach, Florida, with his family in 1957. His younger brother, Greg, took up the guitar, but Duane was so enthralled with the instrument he had Greg teach him how to play. Eventually, the older brother became more proficient on the instrument and the younger boy moved to keyboards.

The two brothers played in a band called The House Rockers, backing up a black vocal group, The Untils. Next, they formed a band called The Allman Joys, recorded a single ('Spoonful'), and began touring the southern club circuit. Eventually, the band broke up and the Allmans formed a new band, Hour Glass, which made it out to California and opened for bands such as The Doors. This band also did not garner much commercial success and broke up. Greg stayed in Los Angles and Duane remained in the south, jamming with several musicians who would eventually become The Allman Brothers.

In 1968 Duane played a session with Wilson Pickett, recording the Beatles 'Hey Jude,' which went on to become a huge hit for Pickett. Duane was then asked to join the Muscle Shoals Rhythm Section, and played on recordings with Aretha Franklin and Boz Scaggs. In 1969 Allman's contract was sold to Capricorn Records. Phil Walden, who ran the company, wanted Allman to put together a band. From various jams, Allman put together a band and asked his brother to join on organ and lead vocals. The Allman Brothers' first album didn't reach very far on the charts, but it established the band's heavyweight instrumental prowess. Twin guitar parts, harmonized leads played by Allman and Dickey Betts, became the signature sound for The Allman Brothers Band.

In the fall of 1970, Duane participated in another session with guitarist Eric Clapton. The album, a one-shot affair, was called *Layla and Other Assorted Love Songs*, and the band was called Derek & The Dominoes. The playing of these two giants of guitar on this record is one for the ages.

Back with The Allman Brothers Band in 1971, Duane recorded a live two-record set called *Live at Fillmore East.* The set featured one of Allman's best recorded examples of slide playing on the opener, 'Statesboro Blues.'

In the fall of 1971, The Allman Brothers returned to the studio. They completed the tracks: 'Stand Back,' 'Blue Sky,' and Duane's lovely acoustic original, 'Little Martha.' Unfortunately, while the band was taking a break from recording, Duane Allman was killed in a motorcycle accident. His legacy lives on, inspiring a new generation of guitarists such as Sonny Landreth and Warren Haynes and pretty much anybody else who decided to play slide guitar after 1969.

Song: 'Statesboro Blues'
Guitar: Gibson SG and Les Paul


Warren Haynes

It wasn't until the early 1990s that The Allman Brothers were able to replace guitarist Duane Allman. The man who would have to fill some mighty big shoes was Warren Haynes. He played in the spirit of Allman but added his own jazz-influenced runs. The Allman Brothers, who had been sagging in popularity, regained much of their lost fan base with Haynes at the helm. Along with founding guitarist Dickey Betts, Haynes was able to meld his blues-based slide playing convincingly with the more melodic approach of Betts. He formed his own band, Gov't Mule, which draws much of its inspiration from Haynes' blues-based playing. At the beginning of the 21st century, Haynes found himself filling some more big shoes, those of Jerry Garcia of The Grateful Dead. With the passing of Garcia, it was thought that the other members of The Dead would hang it up. But just to prove you can't keep a good man down, or a good band down, the remaining members decided to ask Haynes to join them in 2004. A man who seems to breathe new life into once great bands is a man to be reckoned with.

Guitar: Gibson Les Paul

Johnny Winter

Johnny Winter was born February 23rd, 1944, in Beaumont, Texas. Beaumont, at the time, was a city rife with racial tensions and had been the site of one of the worst race riots in Texas history, just nine months before Winter's birth. Businesses were burned and martial law went into effect as 2,000 National Guardsmen and Texas Rangers sealed off the town from the rest of the world. Winter, however, was sincere in his love of blues music, and was welcomed into the black community.

He became friends with Clarence Garlow, a local DJ at the black radio station KJET, who introduced Winter to rural blues and Cajun music. In 1962, the story goes, Winter and his musician brother, Edgar, went to see B.B. King at a local blues club. Edgar and Johnny were the only whites in the crowd, and Johnny wanted to get up on stage and play. King was reluctant, and wanted to see the young man's union card, which Winter showed him. Still not sure about this young white kid, King was finally convinced by several people in the crowd to let the boy play. Winter played, got a standing ovation and King grabbed his guitar back.

Johnny got his breakthrough in 1968, when *Rolling Stone* magazine ran an article on the Texas music scene. A bidding war broke out, won by Columbia Records. On his first album, released in 1969, he covered songs by Robert Johnson, Sonny Boy Williamson II and B.B. King. In addition to recording several more blues-based albums, Winter helped reintroduce blues legend Muddy Waters to a new generation of listeners by producing and playing on three albums in the late 1970s and early 1980s. Waters and Winters friendship evolved to the point that Waters would refer to Johnny as his adopted son.

Winter plays rockin' blues in the Texas tradition, mean and nasty with a lot of swing.

Songs: 'It's My Life, Baby'
Guitar: Gibson Firebird


Lowell George

Between 1969 and 1979, Lowell George, playing with Little Feat and others, built up a reputation as one of the premier slide guitarists of his day. He drew on sources as varied as New Orleans R&B, rock, Latin, Celtic and Asian in his playing. He played on recordings with artists such as John Sebastian, The Meters, Carly Simon and The Grateful Dead.

In the late 1960s, George hooked up with Frank Zappa and the Mothers of Invention, recording two albums, *Cruising with Rueben and the Jets* and *Weasels Rip My Flesh*. He left Zappa's band to form Little Feat in 1971. The band had little success with its first three albums, but 1974's *Feats Don't Fail Me Now* cracked the charts and established George as an incredible slide player. His slide work on 'Rock and Roll Doctor,' 'Oh Atlanta,' and 'Cold, Cold Cold/Triple Face Boogie' are particularly notable.

Little Feat broke up in 1977 and George pursued a solo career. His health, unfortunately, was faltering. Suffering from hepatitis, he nonetheless recorded an album, *Thanks, I'll Eat It Here*, and toured in support of it. During the tour, however, he suffered a heart attack and was pronounced dead on June 29th, 1979.

Compared to Duane Allman's robust slide style, George played more in support of the song. Allman's solos were predominantly blues-based, while George used influences from around the globe to color his playing. He was also an excellent singer and songwriter.

Song: 'Dixie Chicken'
Guitar: Fender Stratocaster


Billy Gibbons


Billy Gibbons, the long-bearded guitarist for ZZ Top, was born on either March 4th or December 16th, 1950 and was raised in and around Houston, Texas. He grew up in a household full of classical and country music, but was transformed – as so many young impressionable musicians of the time were – by an appearance of Elvis Presley on the Ed Sullivan television show. Receiving a Gibson Melody Maker guitar and Fender Champ amplifier for his 13th birthday, the youngster was soon emulating heroes like Little Richard and Jimmy Reed. He played in a series of bands, playing psychedelic rock and pop tunes, during the mid- to late-1960s. Jimi Hendrix, who had Gibbons' band, The Moving Sidewalks, open for him on a Texas tour, called Billy one of his favorite up-and-coming guitarists.

In 1969 he formed a band with bassist Dusty Hill and drummer Frank Beard, forgoing the earlier pop sound for a more straight forward rockin' blues sound. The band was ZZ Top, and it has kept the same lineup since its inception. It released a series of albums in the early- to mid-1970s (including its self-titled debut, *Rio Grande Mud, Tres Hombres, Fandango,* and *Tejas*), becoming one of the country's biggest rock draws. After a three-year hiatus, Top came back in the 1980s with a reworked sound, using sequenced bass, electronic drums and synthesizers. This new direction seem to turn off certain hard-core fans, but led to huge commercial successes such as, 'Legs,' 'Sharp Dressed Man' and 'Give Me All Your Lovin.'"

Some of Gibbons' best slide playing can be heard on the 1974 hit, 'Tush.'

Guitar: Gibson Les Paul
Song: 'Tush'

Ry Cooder

Ry Cooder was given a guitar at the age of ten. It became his driving passion to the exclusion of pretty much anything else. His politically radical upbringing introduced him to the music of Woody Guthrie, and the mythological aspects of Guthrie's concern with the 'dust bowl' and the rural poor striking a strong chord. But it was Delta-style blues which he found even more alluring. He cites 'Dark was the Night, Cold was the Ground' as the inspiration for the memorable theme to his soundtrack for the Wim Wenders' film *Paris, Texas*.

The young native Californian would soak up performances from Sleepy John Estes and Reverend Gary Davis, steeping himself in blues traditions being performed by the last remaining original practitioners of the style.

In his early career he was a sought-after session man, having recorded tracks with The Rolling Stones. In 1970 he recorded his first solo album. Ry Cooder is known for blending myriad traditional sounds into his music, including rural blues, Brazilian and Hawaiian: he traveled to Hawaii to study slack-key guitar with Gabby Pahinui, and spent six months learning the accordion so he could play with Flaco Jimenez, the Mexican master.

Cooder's film score credits include *Southern Comfort, The Long Riders, The Border* and *Paris, Texas*. His sound is haunting, distinctive. His music lends itself so well to film partly because he composes in such a visual manner; one can almost see the rural landscapes of swamps with dark forbidding places, undercurrents of menace in a stark and beautiful landscape. Many modern players cite Ry Cooder as their inspiration for learning slide guitar. They couldn't have a better example of great slide playing. Using heavy-gauged strings and numerous different tunings, Cooder gives the sound the breadth and tone it deserves.

Song: 'Dark is the Night'
Guitars: Gibson Roy Smeck model from the mid 1930s, a 1950s Martin 000-18, Fender Stratocaster.


Bonnie Raitt

Few women have made a name for themselves as guitarists in the blues-rock field. Bonnie Raitt is the exception. Previously lumped in with folkies such as Jackson Browne and The Eagles, Raitt began her recording career in the early 1970s. Initially, she was more highly regarded for her sultry voice than her fine guitar licks.

Raitt, however was raised on the country blues of Mississippi Fred McDowell and the Chicago blues of Muddy Waters. She sought out the old masters, collecting records while still a student at Radcliffe College in Massachusetts. In the late 1960s she quit college and began playing the bar circuit, making it out to California. Her early recordings had some fine slide work and her signature gravelly singing stood out. But she was never mainstream enough for her label, Warner Bros, and so she switched to Capitol, where she flexed her blues muscles.

 It was a good move, because she scored a Number One album with 1989's *Nick of Time*. The album sports the John Hiatt tune, 'Thing Called Love,' featuring Raitt's electric slide work. That same year she walked away with four Grammy awards for *Nick of Time*. The follow-up album, *Luck of the Draw,* featured the hit 'Something to Talk About,' with its lazy slide lines and sexually charged vocal. She has gone on to record collaborations with John Lee Hooker, Roy Orbison and BB King, to name but a few.

Song: 'Something to Talk About'
Guitar: '69 Fender Stratocaster

Roy Rogers

San Francisco Bay Area slide guitarist Roy Rogers has done what few other guitarists have done: made a name for himself by playing exclusively slide guitar. Whether playing his 1970 Martin O-16 acoustic, or his Gibson ES-125, three-quarter scale electric, his music is imbued with the energy of rock and the swampy textures of New Orleans blues.

Born in 1950 in Redding, California, the young Rogers grew up in Vallejo and started playing guitar at age 12. By age 16, he had become increasingly influenced by Delta blues, particularly Robert Johnson. He formed an acoustic duet with harp player David

Burgin in 1973. Later, in 1980, he formed the Delta Rhythm Kings, playing numerous gigs at San Francisco's oldest blues bar, The Saloon. Early in the 1980s, Rogers teamed up with John Lee Hooker and toured for four years with The Coast to Coast Blues Band.

Rogers also went on to produce several albums by Hooker, including *The Healer, Mr. Lucky* and *Boom Boom*. By 1986 he was able to record his first solo album, *Chops not Chaps*. He has gone on to record several solo albums, including the all-instrumental *Slideways*.

He achieves his distinctive sound by running his signal through a chorus pedal with a gain boost. He wears a short slide, which he says leaves the other three fingers free for fretting chords. The sound is amplified by a Mesa Boogie Mark II and a Leslie amp.

Album: *Slideways*
Guitar: Gibson ES-125, Martin 0-16


Sonny Landreth

Sonny Landreth might be considered slightly under the radar as modern slide guitarists go, but that is because he is better known as a sideman in other people's bands, such as those of John Hiatt and Clifton Chenier: he was the first white man to play in Chenier's band. He is, however, not only a great slide player but an accomplished singer and songwriter.

Born in Canton, Mississippi (the home of another great slide player, Elmore James), Landreth moved to Colorado before returning to Mississippi where he joined several Cajun bands, including Beausoleil and Chenier's band. In the 1980s he joined John Hiatt on the songwriting master's *Slow Turning* album. It was here that Landreth really began to make a name for himself, using his wonderful single-string melodies along with a percussive attack that set him apart from many slide players. While his playing has been compared to that of Ry Cooder and David Lindley, his blend of Cajun, rock, and blues gives him a distinctive voice in the slide field.

Tunings: A, A minor, Asus, C, D minor, E, G.
Guitar: Stratocaster.

David Lindley

Similar to Ry Cooder in his eclectic tastes, David Lindley is as much known for his guitar prowess – most notably lap steel type solos – as he is for melding ethnic music such as ska, reggae, African and calypso. He came to the attention of the world through his collaborations with folk artist Jackson Browne. He appeared on several albums by

Browne in the 70s, including *For Everyman* (1973), *Late for the Sky* (1974*), The Pretender* (1976) and *Running on Empty* (1977). The last album helped define his sound with the song 'The Loadout/Stay,' with its lap steel guitar solo resembling a distorted bottleneck.

His 1981 solo project, *El-Rayo X,* kept on the Lindley tradition of eclecticism, but it was the full-throttle 'Mercury Blues' that raced through with more bottleneck-style playing (actually played on lap steel). In addition to working with Jackson Browne, Lindley has been a sideman for Rod Stewart, Linda Ronstadt and Crosby & Nash.

Lindley has a penchant for cheap guitars. He favors Sears Silvertones and funky lap steel guitars to the standard Stratocaster and Les Paul.

Song: 'Mercury Blues'
Guitars: all kinds of weird stuff

SACRED STEEL

In the late 1930s, the electric steel guitar was introduced into the African-American church by brothers Troman and Willie Eason. The instrument has continued to evolve over the past 60 years and has become an incredible voice in gospel music. Powered by spiritual worship and an energy that is infectious, this is a style of slide playing that is woefully under-represented in the secular community. Naturally, the music is played in the service of a 'higher' authority, but even for atheists and agnostics it has a lot to offer, including some of the best slide playing around.

Brought to the attention of the secular world by Chris Strachwitz and Arhoolie Records, the Sacred Steel series has given players like Robert Randolph their own notoriety outside the church service.

The music's geographical center is the state of Florida, but also includes musicians from Seattle, Detroit and Rochester, New York. The leader of the current movement to bring sacred steel players together is Marcus Hardy. Playing his steel guitar at The House of God church in Crescent City, Florida, for groups of a dozen or so holy worshipers, Hardy had a dream to create a community of steel players; one that could share their love of god and music and showcase their talents for each other. In March 2000, his dream came true when the first Annual Sacred Steel Convention was held at Rollins College in Winter Park, Florida.

The image of a steel guitar in a church service for African-Americans seems bizarre, especially since that instrument has become more closely associated with white players and country music. But the instrument, often a replacement for the more common organ, has the ability to whip a congregation into a frenzy. Notable players include Robert Randolph, Aubrey Ghent, and the Campbell Brothers.

Many of the scared steel players utilize an E7 tuning:

Here are some variations on an E and E7 tuning;

| 1 | E  | E  | E  |
|---|----|----|----|
| 2 | B  | B  | D  |
| 3 | G# | G# | B  |
| 4 | E  | E  | G# |
| 5 | B  | D  | E  |
| 6 | E  | B  | B  |

STEEL GUITAR AND COUNTRY MUSIC

When the National and Dobro resonator guitars arrived on the scene in the late 1920s, they were offered in square neck and round neck versions. The round neck style was meant to be played like a regular guitar. The square neck guitars, however, were meant to be played on the player's lap. Soon, electronics began to play a bigger role in amplified music and pickups were added to the guitar. Problems arose with feedback, and so hollow-body guitars were replaced by solid-bodies.

Later, the lap steel evolved into a multi-neck instrument, with two, three, and sometimes four necks. With more physical bulk the instruments became virtually impossible to hold on your lap and so legs were added, thus creating the first 'console' instruments. Strings were added to some of the necks and by the end of World War II the eight-string neck was fairly standard for console style lap steels.

In the early 1950s, players began experimenting with pedals that could raise the pitch of the string. In 1953, Bud Isaacs was the first player to use pedal steel on a hit recording: 'Slowly,' by Webb Pierce. Players would often devise their own tunings, but eventually E9 (Nashville tuning) and C6 (jazz) tuning seemed to become the standard and are probably the most popular setups today. Steel guitars have also evolved into 10- and even 12-string necks.

Important players: Speedy West, Pete Drake.

GUIT-STEEL

Junior Brown

41

"A lot of people tell me they don't like country music, but they like what I am doing," says Junior Brown of Austin, Texas. This seems a bit ironic, since his playing is steeped in old time country flavor. However, with Brown's hyper-kinetic 'guit-steel' playing, he also blends in the energy of rock'n'roll. The guit-steel was born in 1985 after Brown, who had been moving back and forth between lap steel and guitar while singing, decided he needed to wed the two. "I had this dream that the two just kinda melted together. When I woke up, I thought 'You know, that thing would work!' They make double-neck guitars and double-neck steels, so why not one of each?"

A double-neck guitar, the guit-steel combines the best of both worlds: the six-string guitar part is set up just like a Telecaster, and the steel part is an eight-string steel tuned to a C13 chord: Bb, C, E, G, A, C, E, G, low to high. Brown combines classic country lap steel runs with classic Telecaster sounds in his set. He was voted: Number One lap steel player, Number Two country artist and Number Three country album in *Guitar Player*'s 1994 polls.

He began playing music in the early 1960s and by the end of the decade, still a teenager, he turned professional. His father was a piano player and there was always music in the house. His hero, at an early age, was Ernest Tubb, whom he later honored in his song, 'My Baby Don't Dance to Nothing But Ernest Tubb.' Brown was able to meet Tubb on several occasions and his advice to his young protégé was "keep it country."

In the 1980s, Brown was teaching guitar under Leon McAulliffe, the legendary steel player for Bob Wills' Texas Playboys, at Oklahoma's Hank Thompson School of Country Music, part of Rogers State College. It was here that he met the "lovely Tanya Rae" who would become his rhythm guitarist and wife.

Tanya Rae and Junior moved to Austin, Texas, where the musical lines between various styles are a bit blurry. In Brown's set you will hear a lot of old time country, naturally, but you will also hear influences of surf and a bit of Jimi Hendrix. (It seems that once slide playing broke into two camps, bottleneck and lap steel, there developed lines that weren't crossed. The lap steel players created their own tunings and phrasing, while the bottleneck players pretty much stuck to what they had been doing.) Brown's playing, while not combining the two techniques, seems to open the door to a hybrid style of playing, where blues mixes effortlessly with country.

You can hear Brown rippin' it up on several CDs, but 1994's *Guit With It* is perhaps his best, with its great playing, Junior's wry wit ('You're Wanted By The Police And My Wife Thinks You're Dead') and lovely vocal interplay with Tanya Rae.

SLIDE GUITAR TODAY

Ben Harper, Derek Trucks, Alvin Youngblood Hart, Kelly Joe Phelps, Roy Rogers, Sonny Landreth, Martin Simpson, Li'l Ed Williams


Slide guitar today is represented by a host of great players who have used the style to embellish upon songwriting and evoke the textures of a rural past. Ben Harper, Alvin Youngblood Hart and Kelly Joe Phelps are artists who use a myriad of styles to create excellent songs; slide guitar is just one of the choices they make in creating sonic portraits. There are, however, still the virtuosi of slide guitar, those who have made a name for themselves based strictly on their abilities as slide players: Roy Rogers and Sonny Landreth. There is also the Celtic-influenced playing of Martin Simpson and the traditional blues sound of L'il Ed Williams.


Alvin Youngblood Hart

Some call him the Cosmic American Love Child of Howlin Wolf and Link Wray, but it is his interpretations of old rural blues that have earned Alvin Youngblood Hart the highest praise from artists such as Eric Clapton and Ben Harper. His debut recording *Big Mama's Door* in 1996 proved that the waters of the Mississippi Delta ran deep in this young man. Born in 1963, he played songs from the repertoire of Charlie Patton and Robert Johnson like they were second nature to him.

Since the release of his first CD, he has gone on to record several other outings that keep pushing the boundaries of roots music. He is just as likely these days to pick up an electric guitar with tons of distortion as he is to pick up an acoustic and evoke the ghosts of Mississippi's past.

He was born in Oakland, California but moved all over the United States. As he puts it, "three high schools in three time zones." He spent seven years in the Coast Guard; three years as a grunt seaman on a buoy tender on the Lower Mississippi River, and three years as an electronics technician at a radio transmitter station on the West Coast. His electronics background has proved handy for fixing amplifiers in his wife's Memphis guitar shop.

Even though Hart seems to shrug off his label as a blues revivalist, he constantly receives accolades from the blues society at large. In 1997, he received the W.C. Handy award for best new blues artist. His 1998 release, *Territory*, received the *Downbeat* critics' poll award for best blues album – even though it wasn't a blues album. He also received the BBC's award of blues record of the year for his 2000 release, *Start With the Soul*. In 2003 he was nominated for a Grammy.

Song: 'Joe Friday'

Guitars: various

Ben Harper

Ben Harper is a true 21st century journeyman. His music combines funky-soul and jam-band sensibilities with craftsmanlike attention to detail in songwriting. A native of California, Harper grew up listening to blues, folk, soul, R&B and reggae. He started playing guitar as a youngster, and soon became proficient at acoustic slide, which has become his signature instrument. He is one of the few musicians today who plays a Weissenborn guitar: a lap-style guitar made of wood, with a hollow neck.

Playing steady gigs in the Los Angeles area, Harper scored a deal with Virgin records and released his first album *Welcome to the Cruel World* in 1994. His sophomore effort *Fight for Your Mind* was a politically heavy-hitting album with more musical experimentation.

In addition to his solo recordings, Harper has recorded with blues star John Lee Hooker and blues-rockers Gov't Mule.

Guitar: Weissenborn lap-style

Kelly Joe Phelps

Originally, Kelly Joe Phelps started playing slide guitar lap-style on a dreadnought guitar tuned to open D: DADF#AD. After a while he abandoned slide guitar all together. Upon returning to the style he shifted into open G tuning: DGDGBD, and started playing bottleneck-style on a National Style O guitar. This guitarist/singer/songwriter is nothing if not original. His playing and songwriting are filled with virtuosity, mystique and evocative styling that comes across like an impressionist painting. There is a blur between lyric and musical phrasing; one seems to color the other, but neither can rest on its own. The two combine to register on our senses in such a way that the whole leaves us in state of suspension. Listening to Kelly Joe Phelps, one is challenged to interpret his musical offerings in a very personal way.

Raised in the state of Washington, Phelps learned country and folk music, as well as piano and drums from his father. He soon began to concentrate on free jazz and came under the influence of such artists as Miles Davis, Ornette Coleman, and John Coltrane. In the 1980s he focused on acoustic blues and was inspired by players like Mississippi Fred McDowell and Robert Pete Williams.

'The House Carpenter,' from his 1999 release *Shine Eyed Mister Zen*, highlights Phelps's unique slide playing of his earlier career. The sound is pure wood, but the technique employed (lap-style) gives the song a different sound to traditional acoustic-style slide playing. He employs an alternating bass and finger-picking techniques. String-damping is critical to Phelps' style of playing. He plays in open D tuning: D A D F# A D, low to high.

When Kelly Joe returned to slide playing he adopted the bottleneck-style, and with his guitar tuned to an open G chord he started experimenting with playing notes "behind" the slide. A good example of this new style of playing can be heard on the song "Spit Me Outta the Whale" from the 2012 release *Brother, Sinner and the Whale.*
Songs: 'The House Carpenter' 'Spit Me Outta the Whale'
Guitar: Gibson J-60, National Style O


Martin Simpson

A beautiful voice in the world of acoustic fingerstyle guitar, Martin Simpson has continually added new colors to his palette, expanding on his primary interests in British, Anglo-American, and Afro-American traditional forms. Born May 1953 in Lincolnshire, England, Simpson started playing professionally in 1971. He recorded his first album, *Golden Vanity*, in 1976 and within a year he was opening shows for bands such as Steeleye Span. Through the years he has recorded many collaborations with singer June Tabor. In 1987 he moved to the United States and has lived there since.

In his music, Simpson has drawn on the inspiration of artists such as Henry Cox and Blind Willie Johnson and Blind Willie McTell, as well as Bob Dylan and Richard Thompson. Martin's music is a reflection of both British and US regional influences. Simpson's playing is economical, concentrating his effort on making each note count. His slide playing is clean and articulate, substituting purity of soul for histrionics.

Song: 'Greenfields Of Canada'
Guitar: Sobell acoustic

Li'l Ed Williams
Li'l Ed and the Blues Imperials have been dubbed "the world's number one houserocking band." Williams, whom some would call 'petite' is, however, a giant among blues slide players. Hailing from the West Side of Chicago, Williams boasts a direct bloodline to the great slide player, J.B Hutto (his uncle and musical mentor). The band is a favorite at blues festivals throughout the United States, and thanks to Williams' gifted vocals and on-stage flamboyance – a penchant for duck-walking and back-bending – has become a top blues act.

Born in 1955, Ed was surrounded by the blues. He was playing guitar, drums, and bass by the time he was 12 years old. Ed claims that his uncle, J.B Hutto, "taught me everything I know." By 1975 he had formed the first incarnation of The Blues Imperials, playing every West Side club at night while he worked ten hours a day at a car wash. The band released its first album *Roughhousin'* in 1986. Since then Ed hasn't looked back to his car wash days.

As can be guessed, the Imperials play good-time-music and Ed's slide playing is a spirited amalgam of the styles of Chicago blues players like Elmore James and J.B. Hutto. Turn it up, get down and let it ride!

Song: 'Never Miss Your Water'
Guitar: Gibson ES-335

Derek Trucks

Many consider Derek Trucks the modern day hero of slide guitar. His pedigree is strong; uncle, Butch Trucks was one of the founding members of the Allman Brothers Band. He sights his early influences as Duane Allman and Elmore James, but has gone on to be inspired by everyone from Django Reinhardt to Miles Davis, and he even studied Indian music at the Ali Akbar College of Music in San Rafael, CA. he has been a member of the Allman Brothers band and is a founding member of the Tedeschi Trucks Band, along with wife, Susan Tedeschi.

Trucks style has been influenced by a wealth of blues and eastern sounds and his playing is unique with the blending of pentatonic and middle-eastern influenced scales.

He plays a Gibson SG through two vintage Fender Super Reverb amps. He most often plays in Open E Tuning (EBEG#BE) and uses a Dunlop Blues Bottle slide.

# CHAPTER 2:
## OPEN G TUNING

*In this chapter we will:*

- *Learn about materials and technique*
- *Learn how to get to G tuning from standard tuning*
- *Learn scales and licks for slide in open G tuning*
- *Learn a shuffle rhythm in open G*
- *Learn several other rhythm grooves*
- *Learn some solos in open G*
- *Learn "Death Letter Blues" and "Terraplane Blues."*
- *Learn a walking bass line and groove*
- *Combine slide licks with finger style playing in open G Tuning*

Today slides come in all sorts of exotic shapes and sizes – some even rather suggestive. One's choice of slide is a bit of a personal decision. However, here are some tips for what kind of slide might best suit your needs. Keep in mind that you will probably want to buy a small assortment of slides to experiment with.

You can choose from metal/brass, glass or ceramic slides – there might be other materials out there but these are the best. Glass tends to be a little smoother than metal but some people say metal is louder. I like the sound of brass, but unless the brass stays polished it has a tendency to get a little 'sticky.' These days I prefer ceramic, it seems to combine the best qualities of both metal and glass; it slides better on the string with a consistent pressure. The metal slides are thinner and therefore a bit easier to direct and get accuracy directly over the fret. If you go for glass I recommend a thicker glass to the thinner variety: thinner glass slides have a tendency to sound thin. You can also use household objects such as a socket from a socket wrench set or the cut-off top of a wine bottle (a blues classic!)

Placement: Most players place the slide on their pinky; this gives you the most flexibility, allowing the other fingers freedom to fret other strings and make chords. There are, of course, many players (some of them presented in this book) who place the slide on their ring, middle or even their index finger! The slide should fit snuggly and you can compensate for a loose fitting slide by stuffing some foam or candle wax into it.

As your slide touches the string keep in mind that you don't need to apply too much pressure to the string: it's more important to keep *consistent* pressure as you slide from note to note. The slide should only cover the string(s) that you are playing slide notes on. For instance, if you are playing notes on the high E-string you should only cover that one string with the slide. A lot of slide playing occurs on the high E-string, and here are a couple points for getting good sound. First, you are covering just the E-string with your slide. As you move from note to note keep consistent pressure on the string. Finally, tilt the slide slightly away from you and the fretboard; thus avoid hitting other strings and nasty overtones.

String Dampening:

A critical aspect of slide playing is string dampening, which can be achieved with both hands. There are times when you want string noise and overtones and there are times when you don't want it. These tips are for those times when you don't want it. First, as you drag the slide across the strings use one or more of the fingers of your left hand to touch and drag along that string with the slide. I use my index finger, which results in a slight 'cupping' of my hand. This technique will rid you of some unsound string overtones. The cupping of the hand also tends to consolidate your hand, making it feel as if it is one appendage moving rather than five independent digits. Also, in conjunction with your thumb planted behind the neck it helps you to get more of a 'swirling' rotation of your wrist as you move from note to note.

You can also use the palm of your right hand (forgive me, lefties!) to dampen notes. I often rest the palm of my right hand on the bass strings if I am playing slide notes on the higher strings. After I play the note on, for instance, the G-string and slide, then move to the B-string, my palm would descend to the G-string to deaden that string.

# __Introduction to G Tuning__

Tuning the guitar to an open chord is one of the best ways to get the most out of bottleneck slide playing. Not only can you place your bottleneck across all the strings to get chords up and down the neck, but the open strings can also be a great ally as you improvise and build solos. You also have multiple octaves (two Gs, and three Ds).

To get to G tuning from standard tuning: start by lowering your E (6$^{th}$) string a whole step to D. Next, lower the A (5$^{th}$) string a whole step to G. Finally, Tune the high E (1$^{st}$) string down a whole step to D. This will put you at:

| D   | G   | D | G | B | D  |
|-----|-----|---|---|---|----|
| 6↓  | 5↓  | 4 | 3 | 2 | 1↓ |

You now have only 3 notes: GBD, which make up a major triad. You will notice that unlike D tuning (which we will cover in the next chapter), the root note for the bass is on the 5$^{th}$ string. This makes G tuning slightly more challenging for fingerpickers because we have to use an "inner" string in order to get a steady dead thumb or alternating bass pattern. Also, the first string gets used a lot in slide playing; in D tuning we have an open root on the first string, but in G tuning we don't get to the root until the 5$^{th}$ fret.

The following exercises and examples will lead you through several rhythm grooves, a few solos* and some solo fingerpicking exercises and songs. The recording will give you a chance to hear the solo both in context with the rhythm and without. The CD also has a solo rhythm track for you to practice against.

\*

# Scales in open G

The following scales can be used in the exercises and solos throughout this chapter

**G Minor pentatonic scales on open G Strings**

**...on 2nd (B string)**

**..on open D strings (1st, 4th, 6th)**

**Two octave G minor pentatonic**

# First Open G Slide exercises
## open G: DGDGBD

Beginning Open G Exercises

In exercise 1 we will practice simply moving the slide between scale tones of the minor pentatonic. Make sure to keep your slide low, just covering the 1st string. Timing here is not important. Just getting a good, even sound, using your damping finger.

In exercise 2 we will use the same pentatonic scale but work the 3rd string. This will require you to "dip" the slide in. It's okay to cover the 1st and 2nd string as well, but be conscious of the sound: if its not pleasing to you, then you might need to angle the slide in so that you are not touching the 1st or 2nd strings.

In exercise 3 and 4 we get the chance to play multiple strings. Its important to make sure your slide is NOT tilted so that all the strings have an even sound.

Exercise 5 gives us a chance to vary the length of the slide notes. The first few notes are quick, but then the slide lingers a little longer over the 2nd string slide between the 10-12th fret. This will be something you will want to keep in mind as you develop your slide playing: long vs. short, decay vs. sustain and when to cut the note off with either your left or right hand (more on this later).

Exercise 6 – speaking of long and short; the next example is an exercise in playing long and short slide notes. We will cover the same territory – between the 3rd and 8th frets – but the first time you will play the slide very quickly and then stop the sound almost immediately (use your right hand palm or your left hand damping finger). The second time you will elongate the note; taking your time getting from the 3rd fret to the 8th fret. Notice the contrast

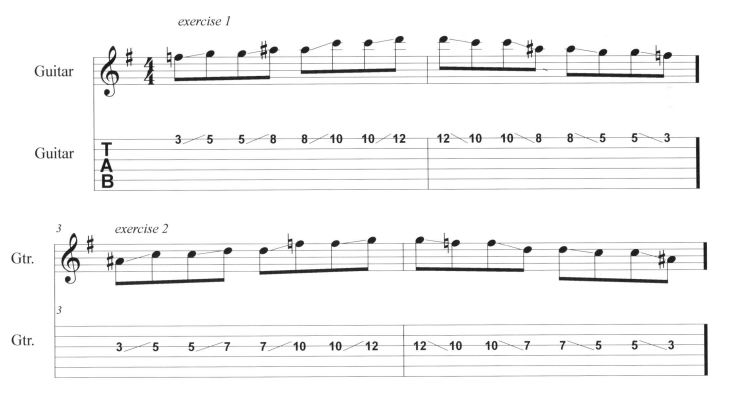

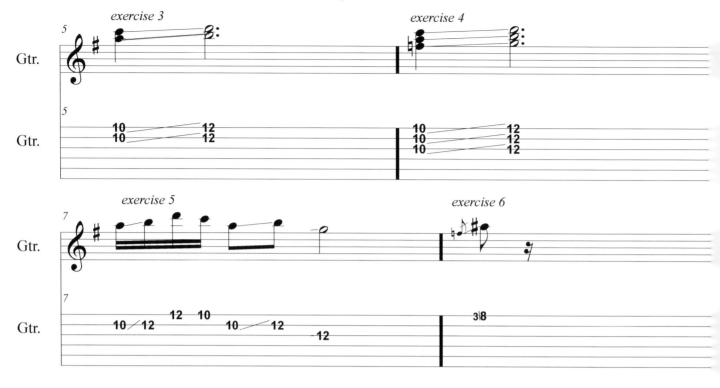

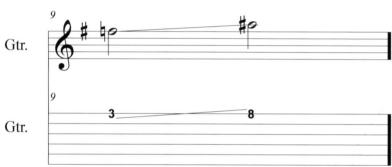

# Open G Blues shuffle

pete

Let's create a background for some slide licks in G Tuning. The shuffle rhythm is ubiquitous in blues and its important to be able to play it correctly. The shuffle can be played fast or slow. If you play it fast you should use you right hand plam to mute the strings. It's a great idea to record yourself playing this rhythm so you can play some licks like those on the following page over it. The solo on the next page should be played over this rhythm.

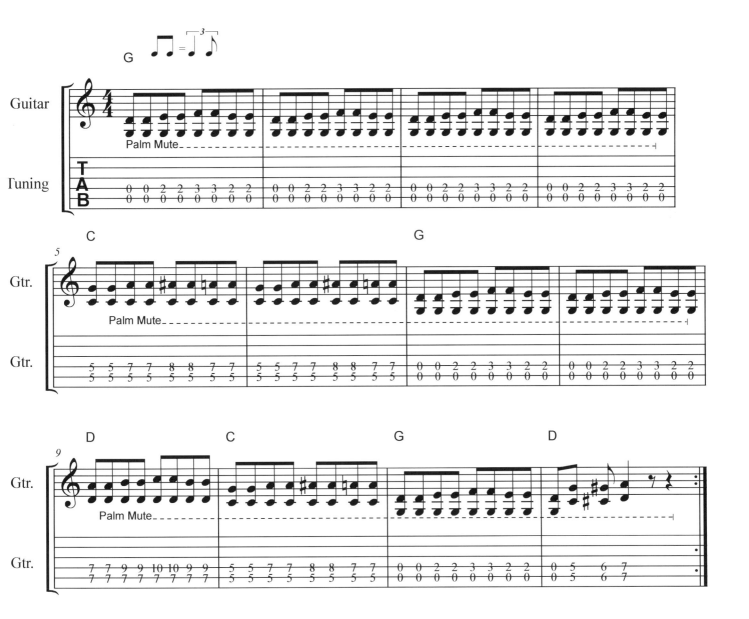

# Solo for open G Shuffle:

Pete Madse

This solo demonstrates a couple of good ideas for open G. The first 4 bars are played over a G chord. Basically, this portion of the solo travels between G octaves: high G on the 1st string 5th fret, down to the open 3rd string G. When the the progression travels to C and D you can simply follow the chords to the 5th and 7th frets respectively, working your slide licks above and below those frets.

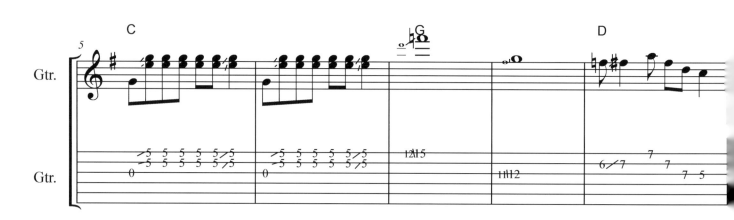

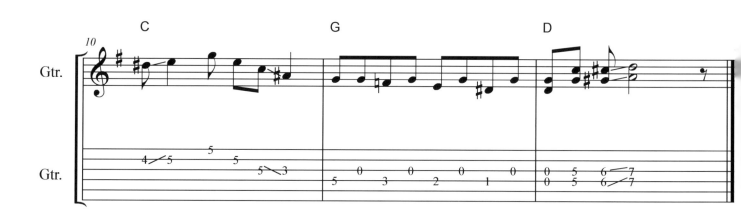

# Slide Etude in G tuning

## DGDGBD

The rhythm groove in this example gives you a chance to practice a monotonic bass with some cool sounding chords. The first G chord voicing(s) are charateristic of Robert Johnson. The C7 chord in measure 5 looks like a normal C chord, but because we are in G tuning it places a Bb in the bass giving this chord a very nice sound.

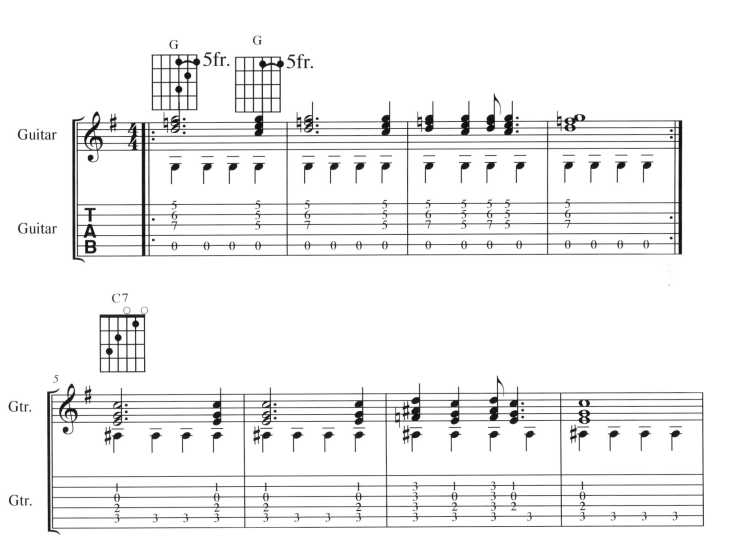

Slide Etude in G tuning

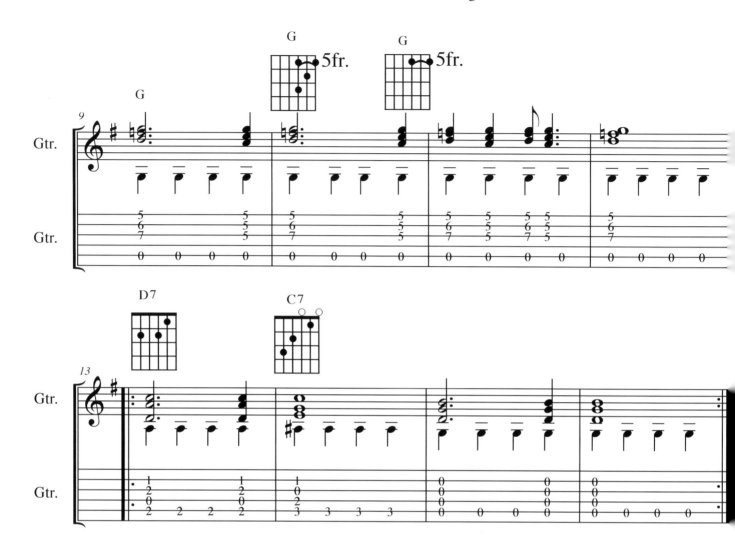

# Slide Etude in G tuning
## ~SOLO~

The solo here is intended to be played over the preceeding "Slide Etude" groove. The beginning of this solo gives you some practice at playing some inner strings. Remember to try and tilt your slide in a little. Double-stops in measure 5, and an octave (played on the 1st and 4th string) in measure 8 are new -- your slide will need to cover the top four strings.
Another octave run in measure 11 and 12 should be played with the bottleneck, even though you are not sliding.

Tuning: DGDGBD

Slide Etude in G tuning

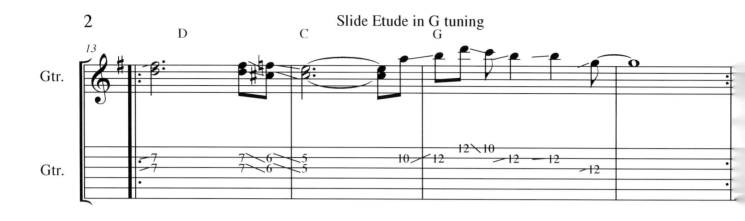

# Muddy Waters Style

Open G: DGDGBD

**pete**

For this exercise in open G tuning you can keep the tone pretty clean. Muddy did a lot of slide playing on the bass strings and that's where the emphasis lies. This exercise is mainly pick or right-hand thumb based, but in measure five you start to use some simultaneous bass and melody notes. If you are holding a flat pick you can simply pick the bass notes and use your ring finger to play the melody notes. In this piece you can hear a synthesis of rural and city sounds. There is a little more drive in the music but you can still hear a hint of rural 'bounce."

# Open G w/Bass

This exercise is designed to be played without the accompaniment. We start to blend in bass notes that establish a background rhythm within the context of the solo. The last two bars are typical of a Robert Johnson-style turnaround in G tuning.

# "Boogie on a Roll"

OPEN G TUNING:
DGDGBD

This is one I made up to have some fun playing slide in G tuning. It employs some ideas from Robert John-
Son House and probably a few others.

# SLIDE AND BEYOND
## In G Tuning: DGDGBD

The purpose of this workshop is to learn a few rhythmic and expressive devices used by players like Robert Johnson and Son House and explore some other ideas that are available to us in G tuning. We will play a bit of bottleneck slide, but the focus will be on rhythm, groove and exploration of what this tuning offers us in a bluesy setting.

SON HOUSE AND ROBERT JOHNSON LICKS AND RIFFS:

Let's start with some fairly well-known songs. Son House's "Death Letter Blues" is an open G slide song that uses a monotonic bass pattern: single string bass played on the downbeat. The only slide phrases that House actually plays in this song are in the first measure and repeated throughout. These consist of a quick slide on the first upbeat (on the 3rd and 4th strings) and on the second upbeat on the first string. This lick actually has double-duty as it is also integral to Robert Johnson's "Walking Blues." This is great place to start if you have never played slide in open G. The target note here is the G played on the first string at the 5th fret.

The rest of "Death Letter..." is barred chords (C and D) played at the 5th and 7th frets respectively. These are non-slide chords and should be played with your first finger barring the 1-5th strings. Of course, since you have a slide on your pinky you will have to stretch your ring finger up to the 8th fret/C or 10th fret/D – for those of you who have seen photos or videos of Johnson and House it will be pretty clear that having long fingers helps in this process!

"Terraplane Blues" has a wonderful rhythmic pattern that Johnson plays over the G chord. In the first 4 bars of the verse he comes back again and again to this really cool chord voicing that looks like a minor triad (if it was in standard tuning), But this "slanted" chord shape is really a 7th chord. He would bounce between this chord and a partial barre at the 5th fret that covers the top three strings, as well as open strings. In the fourth bar of this example he uses single strings, 1st string/5th fret (G) and 1st string/3rd fret (F) to bounce back and forth between the G and G7 chords.

# Death Letter Blues

## G Tuning: DGDGBD

Son House

arr: Pete Madsen

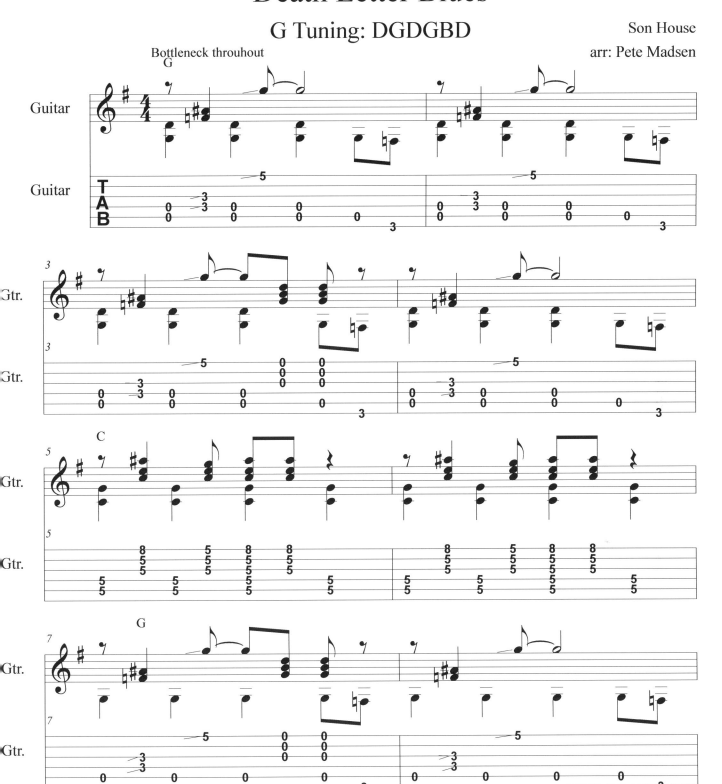

66

2

Death Letter Blues

ALTERNATE FIRST FOUR BARS

*Walking bass played with thumb over neck*

67

# Terraplane Blues

**Robert Johnson**
Pete Madsen

Terraplane Blues

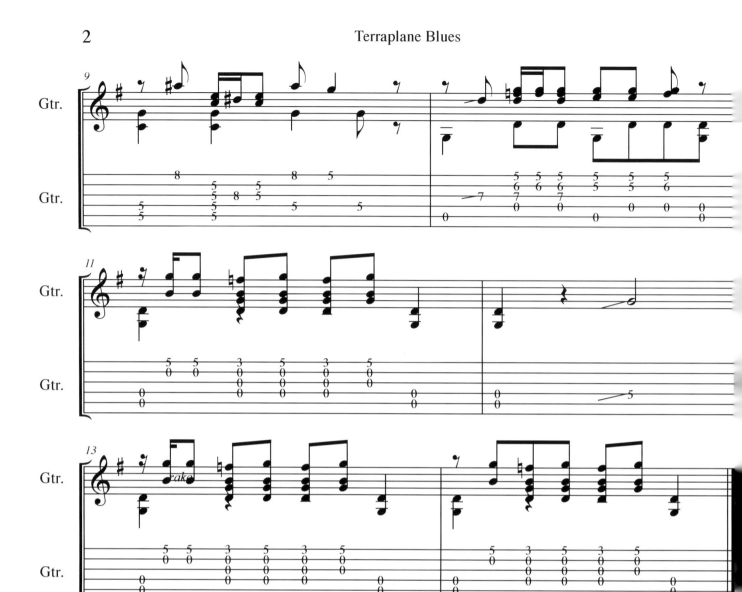

# Walking with My Baby Blues
## in open G Tuning:DGDGBD

### EXPLOITING THE FLAT 7TH

Much of blues playing, both rhythmically and in lead playing, revolves around dominant 7th chords. A dominant 7th chord is made up of the root, 3rd, 5th and flatted 7th of a major scale. The sound of the flatted 7th is significantly different from the major 7th. I think of the major 7th as having a very pretty sound; whereas the flat 7th sounds a bit off-kilter, unresolved and creates a dynamic tension in the sound.

We saw this in Terraplane Blues with the G7 chord that Johnson plays.

In "Walking with My Baby Blues" we will be using the 7th chord tonality and surrounding it with a walking bass line. At first, you might want to try this without the slide on your finger. Start by fretting the first string/3rd fret with your middle finger (this is the flat 7th/F). You will then play the walking bass line with your index and ring fingers. For the most part the bass line is played on the downbeat and the 7th chord voicing on the upbeat – although on the 3rd beat I sneak in an extra bass note! This covers the first four measures. Once we have established this groove we can start to play with it a bit.

As we begin measure 5 it sounds like we are repeating the original riff but then we add in a little twist: we throw in the tonality of a flatted 2nd interval (B flat against B). At first this might sound "off," but as you work it up to speed it will sound cool and "quirky."

In measure 9 we come to our IV chord (C) and once again build a walking bass line around a 7th chord. Note: the shape of this chord looks identical to the shape of a C7 chord in standard tuning, but on closer inspection that note played on the 5th string at the 3rd fret, which is normally a C in standard tuning, is actually a B flat (the flat 7!)

In measure 13 we play the V chord (D) and use a descending double-stop lick played on the 3rd and 2nd strings – you might notice that the double-stop on the 5th fret and the one played on 1st and 2nd frets are, again, 7th chords. One thing I like about playing in open G tuning is that you can navigate the 2-4th strings like you would normally in standard tuning. So the lick I just played under the D chord could be used in standard tuning, as well, to similar effect.

In the next section of this song/exercise I have come up with several call and response ideas that use the original walking bass riff. When you play through these think of them as matching pairs: one bar bass riff/one bar response. The first "response" is borrowed from our Robert Johnson riff in "Terraplane Blues." The second response is a very fast cascading lick that sounds cool and isn't too difficult to play. The third is a nice little slide lick. The fourth uses a descending bass line that answers the ascending bass line. The fifth response is a triplet hammer-on. The sixth uses simple harmonics played at the 5th, 7th and 12th frets.

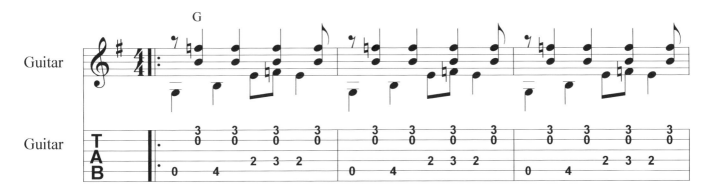

# Texas Honeymoon

## DGDGBD

This one can either be played as a solo or as background accompaniment for slide. For the most part, it's a monotonic bass in open G tuning (DGDGBD). The first 10 bars don't use the bottleneck, but starting on measure 11 the bottleneck will be used as you climb up the neck. In measure 14 there is a nice little chord shape that alternates with some slide riffs. This chord shape will be repeated at the 10th fret.

2

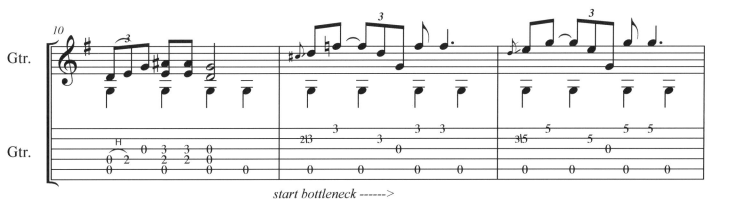

start bottleneck ------>

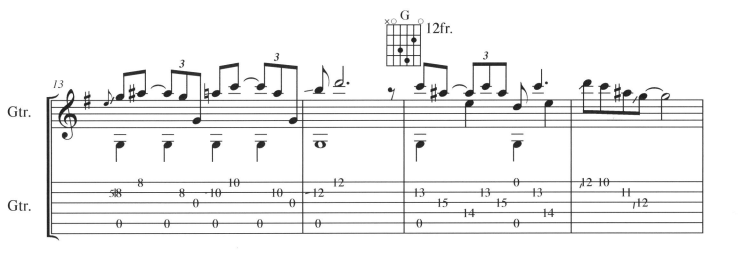

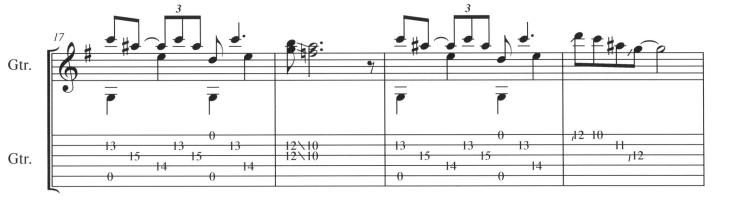

74

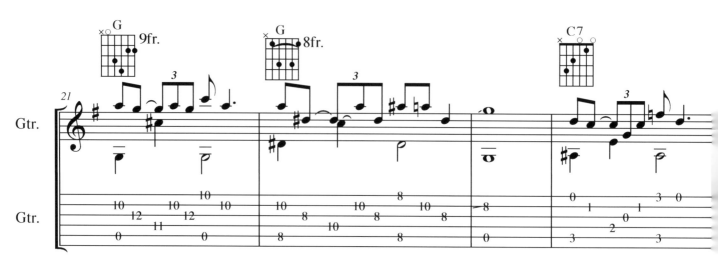

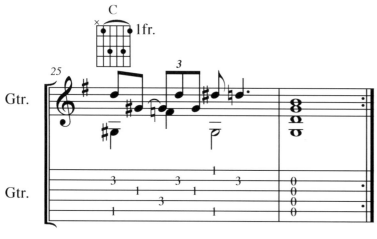

# CHAPTER 3: OPEN D TUNING

*In this chapter we will:*

*• Learn how to get to D tuning from standard tuning*

*• Play a slow haunting song called "The Pass" which will help us with technique and intonation.*

*• Learn scales and licks for slide in open D tuning*

*• Learn a shuffle rhythm in open D*

*• Learn some solos in open D*

*• "Dust My Broom" and "You've Got to Move" -style riffs*

*• Learn some fingerpicking exercises*

*• Learn two fingerpicking songs with alternating bass and slide in D tuning: "Steel Guitar Rag" and "Hope Springs Eternal."*

# INTRODUCTION TO OPEN D TUNING

The most significant aspect to open D tuning is three root notes: the 6th, 4th and 1st strings are all tuned to D. This makes the tonal possibilities intriguing; root notes on open strings can provide drones, great hammer-on and pull-offs and octave runs. Also, if you are a finger picker it is easier to play an alternating or monotonic bass pattern.

To get to open D from standard tuning: drop the 6th string a whole step from E to D. Then drop the 3rd string from G to F#; the second string from B to A, and the first string from E to D: DADF#AD.

| 6 | 5 | 4 | 3 | 2 | 1 |
|---|---|---|---|---|---|
| D↓ | A | D | F#↓ | A↓ | D↓ |

The exercises in this section range from the slow and spooky ("The Pass") to outright party tunes ("Dust My Broom"). In between we have some rhythm exercises some solo ideas, some fingerpicking exercises and a cool tune called "Hope Springs Eternal."

"The Pass" is a good song for working on slide technique.. Take your time with your bottleneck playing. Focus on intonation and using your damping finger.

"Dust My Broom" requires that you drive the rhythm with some triplet runs and shuffle eighth notes. In this instance "clean" slide technique is less important than rhythmic drive. For those of you who are normally very clean players this is an opportunity for you get a little "dirty" and cut loose.

Most everyone has heard the Rolling Stones version of "You've Got to Move," but it was Mississippi Fred McDowell who wrote the tune.

I have include a couple of fingerpicking tunes, including "Steel Guitar Rag" which has us playing single string runs as well as full chords with the slide covering all the strings.

Open D was the first open tuning I learned and to this day I really enjoy playing around with the possibilities. "Hope Springs Eternal" is a culmination of my fingerpicking and slide ideas. This one is a great toe-tapper and is usually played at the end of a set.

# THE PASS

This exercise is a good introduction to slide playing in D tuning: DADF#AD. To get to
D tuning from standard tuning (EADGBE) drop the 6th string one whole step from E to D,
drop the 3rd string 1/2 step from G to F#, drop the 2nd string a whole step from B to A and
drop the 1st string a whole step from E to D. The major challenge of this exercise is to go
from playing single string riffs (1st string) to playing mutiple strings (chords). Play this piece slow,
focusing on your tone and intonation.

# Scales and Riffs in Open D Tuning

Exercise 1 is a minor pentatonic scale played on both the 1st and 2nd strings. You can practice either sliding from note to note or pick up the slide after each note and slide one fret below the target note; e.g. slide from the 3rd fret to the 5th fret, or slide from the 2nd → 3rd fret, then take the slide off the string and place it at the 4th fret as you slide into the 5th fret. Remember, when you take the slide off the string your damping finger is the last thing to remove otherwise you can get some unintended noise.

*exercise 1*

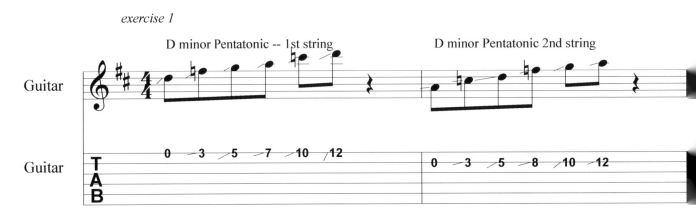

In exercise 2 we will do the same thing but with a Dorian scale. This scale has seven notes instead of five but still has a minor sound.

*exercise 2*

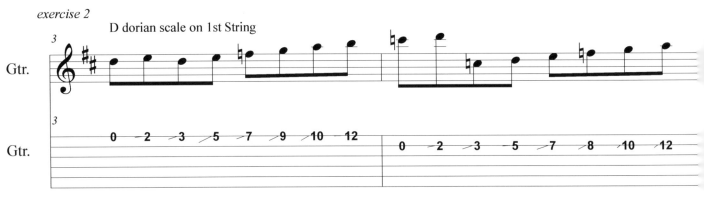

For exercise 3 you can take off the slide or leave it on, but the notes you will be playing are all fretted. These are parallel thirds: interval of thirds played on adjacent strings. Adding this in to your catalog of riff will provide a great accompaniment to you slide playing.

*exercise 3*

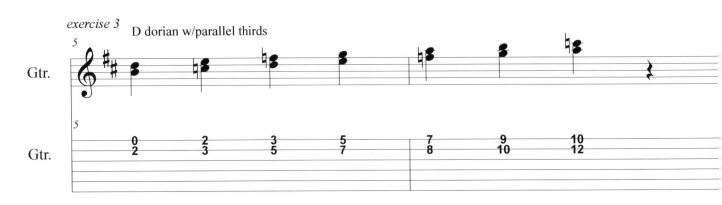

Exercise 4 and 5 are hybrid scales. I like to think of these scales as extensions of the chordal tones played at the 12th fret. The notes at the 12 fret are the same as the open strings: DADF#AD. So when we play at the 10th or 15th fret we are stretching the chordal tones with the idea that we can come back to the 12th fret and play a safe note. Duane Allman would use this kind of scale prodigiously.

Exercise 6 is a classic Dunae Allman-style lick. We use backwards slides on the 2nd and first strings to create some harp-style licks; then slide 11-12th fret on the 3rd string before resolving on the root note (D) on the 4th string/12th fret. This sets up a call and response which is answered in the following measure. This time our lick is played on the bass strings, but resolves to the same note: D.

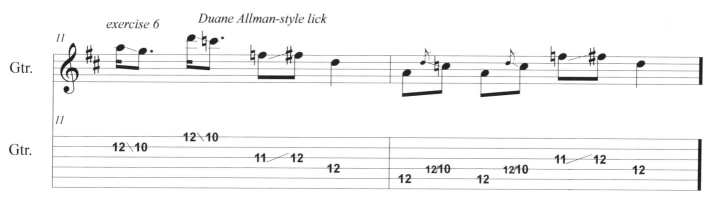

Exercise 7 moves to the 15th fret and then back to the 12th before jumping to the 15th fret to play a chromatic descent back to the 12th on the B (A) string and resolving on the 4th string D note again.

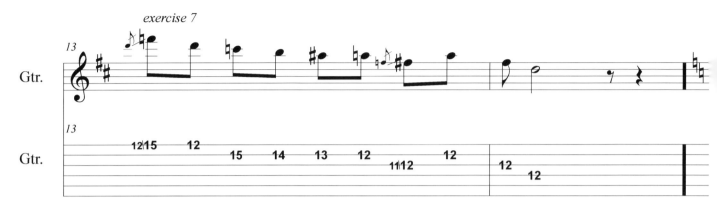

Exercise 8 is similar to the classic "Dust My Broom" riff which was played by Elmore James. Here we are covering multiple strings and cutting loose with a flurry of triplets. Attitude is more important than accuracy on this one. Rhythm is key, though. Counting or tapping out the rhythm can be helpful: each beat has 3 segments which can be counted: "trip–l-et", or "1-2-3, 2-2-3, 3-2-3," or "one-and-a."

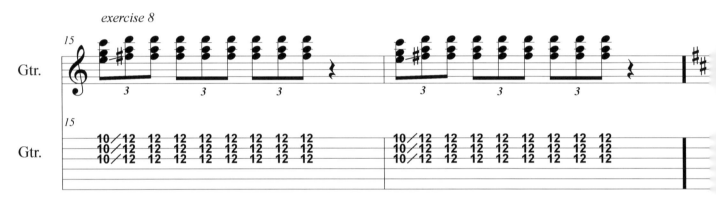

Exercises 9 and 9a forgo the slide and are licks that you should have in you open D pocket of tricks. We use the F note bent up to an F# on the second string to anchor the lick as we play various other notes on the first string that are within reach.

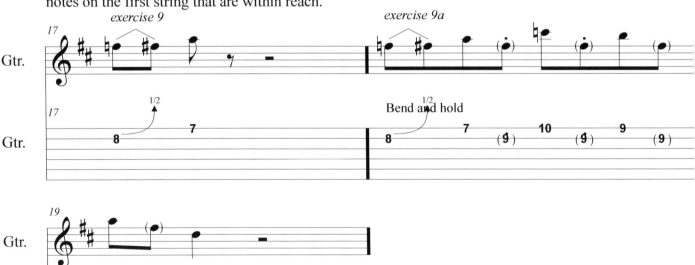

# Rhythm Blues shuffle open D

DADF#AD

Just like the shuffle in open G, you should try recording yourself playing this rhythm so you can play along with it.

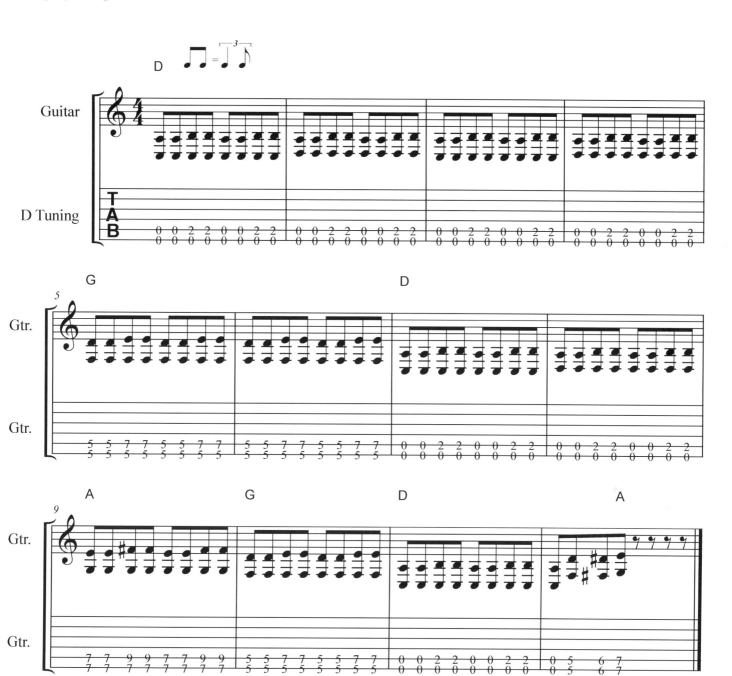

82

# Slide Solo in open D over 12 bar Shuffle

The idea in this solo is to work the area around the 12th fret. Remember, notes played at the 12th fret are the same (only an octave higher) than the open strings. The 12th fret is home base. We can work around that area, play two frets below (10th fret) and three frets above (15th fret). Experiment and see what kind of licks and riffs you can come up with.

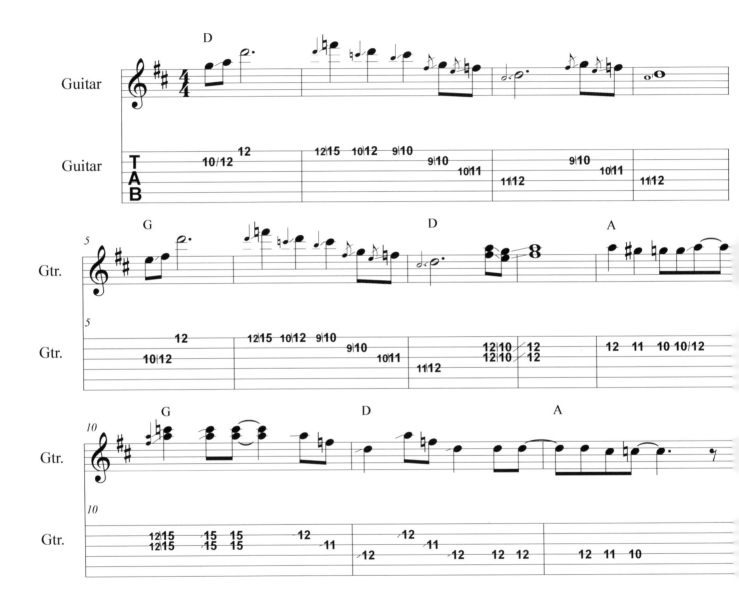

# Open D solo #2

Here is another slide solo in open D which spans two 12 bars. Lots of open strings throughout this piece. One of the advantages to playing in an open tuning is the use of lots of open strings. However, moving from string to string with slide notes in between can lead to some unwanted noise via the slide being taken off and placed back on the strings. This is where the damping finger plays a critical role. Remember, for the damping finger: first thing on/last thing off the string. I'm probably sounding like a broken record, but this really is critical to getting a good sound.

In the second round of twelve bars we create a lick that uses a slightly sharp (#) note played on the 3rd fret of the the first string. If you read the standard notation you might think this note is an F#, but in fact, it's a note somewhere between F-F#. One of the beauties of slide guitar is playing notes that are a microtone or two sharp or flat, thus creating a more vocal-like quality to the sound.

84

# You've Got to Move

OPEN D: DADF#AD

**Fred McDowell**

The slide line in "You've Got to Move" follows the vocal line; it's very similar to the vocal quality of the slide playing of Robert Johnson in "Come On in My Kitchen," which is in G tuning. Notice that you play the melody on the first string; then replay it two octaves lower on the fourth string. This is great way to reinforce a musical statement without sounding too repretitious.

You've Got to Move

# Dust My Broom style groove

OPEN D TUNING: DADF#AD

**Pete**

This version of "Dust My Broom" is as much based on Robert Johnson as it is on Elmore James. Johnson is credited with writing, but he would have played it in open G tuning (DGDGBD). This version is in open D (DADF#AD). There is a nice juxtaposition between the multi-string slide riff and the shuffle rhythm played on the low two strings. This requires jumping back and forth between the nut and the 12th fret. Practice this move so that you can do it quickly and accurately.

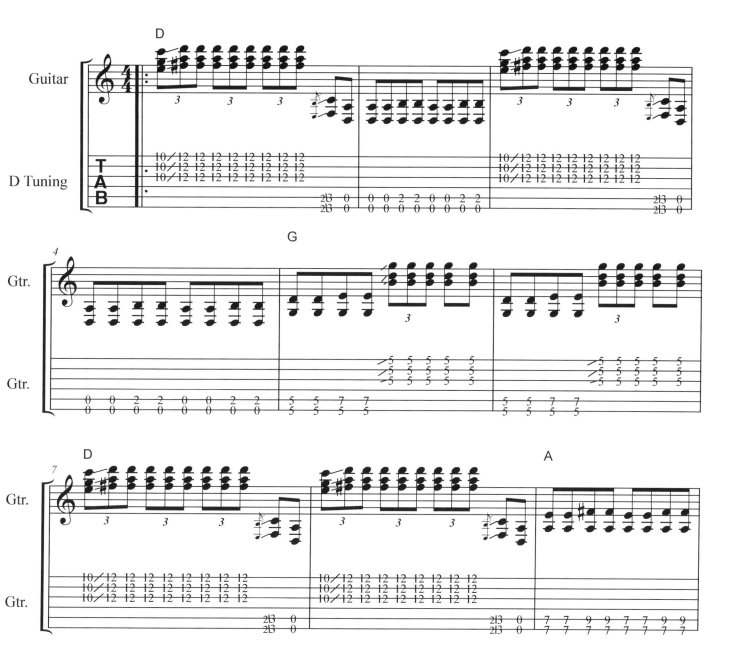

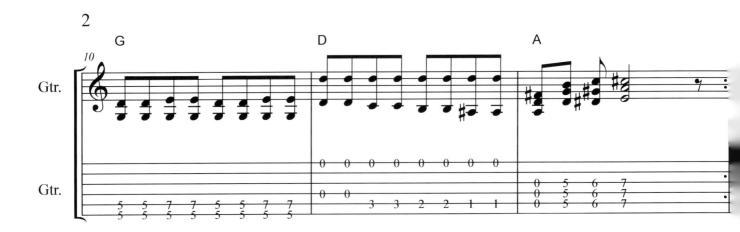

# Fingerpicking exercises

## OPEN D: DADF#AD

Playing in open tunings is a great opportunity to learn some alternating bass fingerpicking techniques: you can focus on your right hand without being overly incumbered by fingering with your fretting hand. Here I have given you a basic alternating bass that travels between the 6th and 4th string and should be played by your right hand thumb. In the next measure we add two high strings (melody strings). These strings can be played with any combination of right hand index, middle and ring fingers. Most early blues players used only index or index and middle fingers. I use three fingers and thumb when I fingerpick.

The 3rd measure is a dominant 7th scale that will be used in the following measures. When you can navigate this scale with the fingerpicking pattern, try using your slide to play the notes on the 1st string with the fp pattern.

90

# Steel Guitar Rag

## OPEN D TUNING:

### DADF#AD

Here is a good one to practice your slide chops combined with fingerpicking. It's in open D tuning and sounds good at slow or fast tempos.

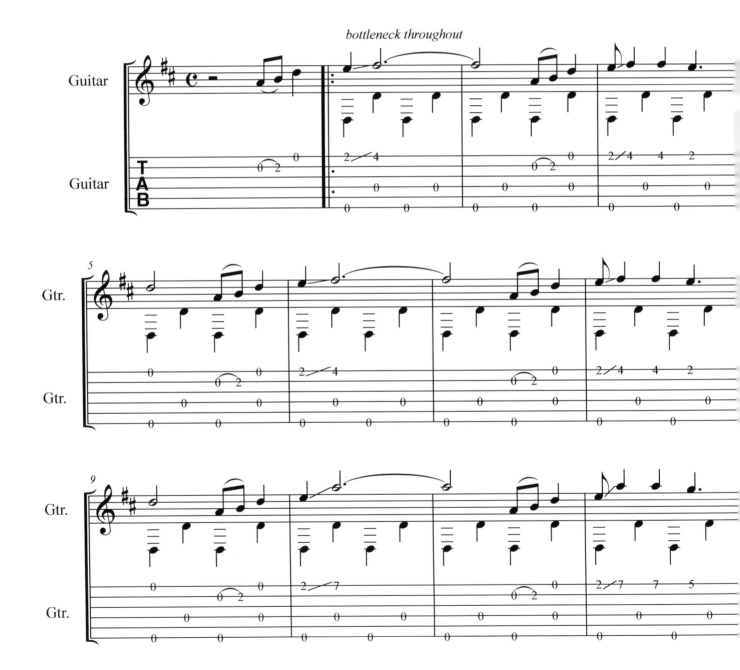

91

2

Steel Guitar Rag

# 4

Steel Guitar Rag

94

# "Hope Springs Eternal"

Pete Madse

Here's one to test out fingerpicking with slide.

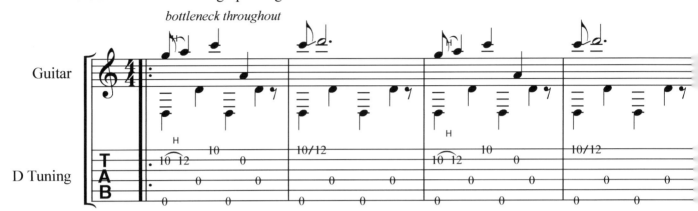

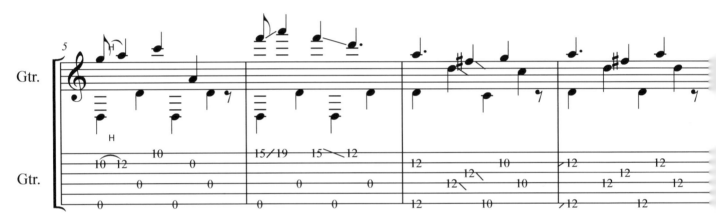

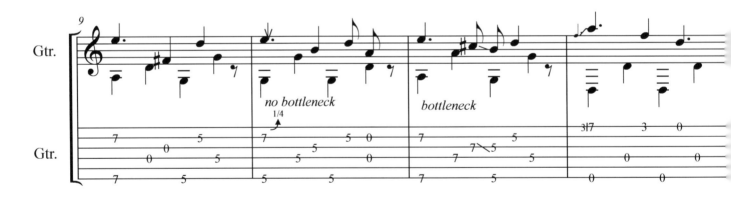

HSE

A

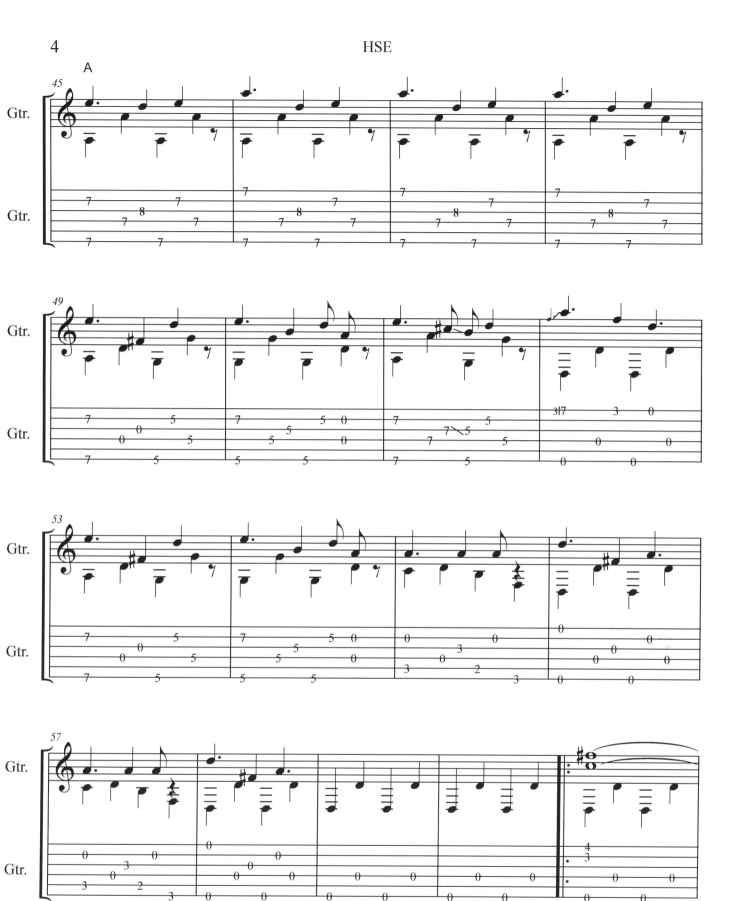

*no bottleneck*

*BRIDGE*

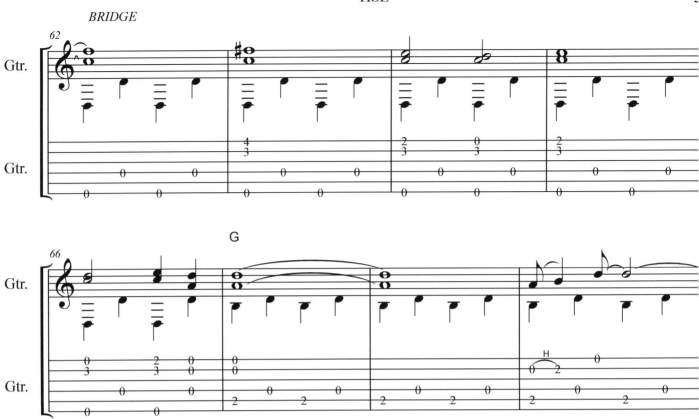

G

D

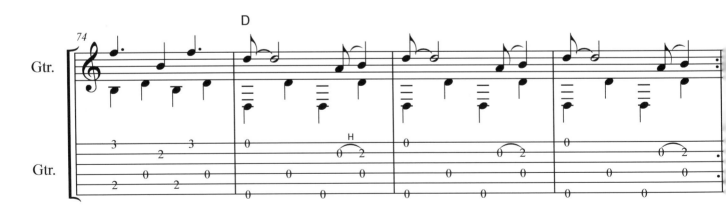

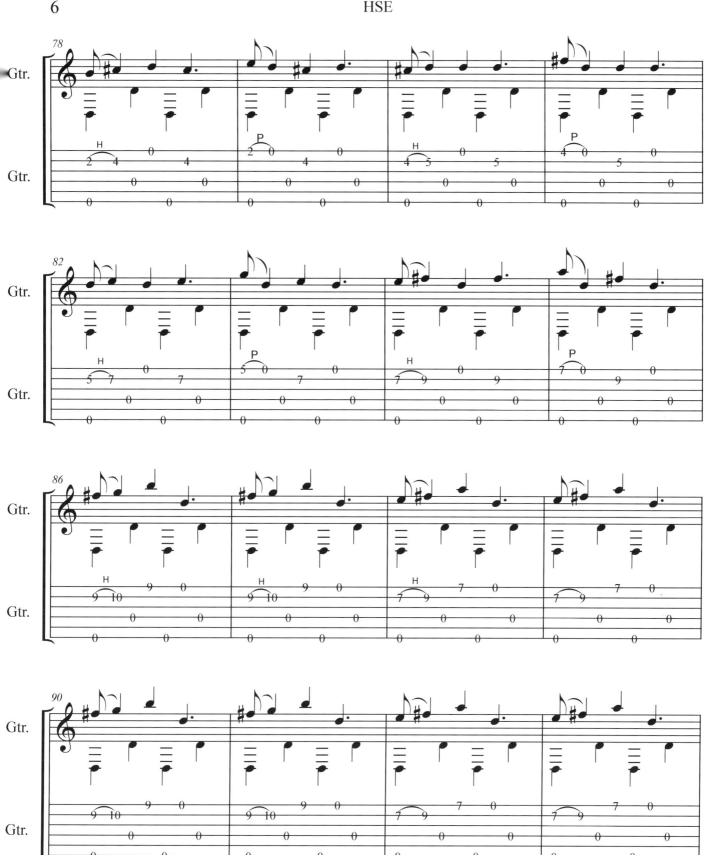

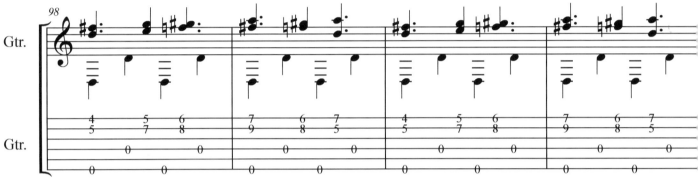

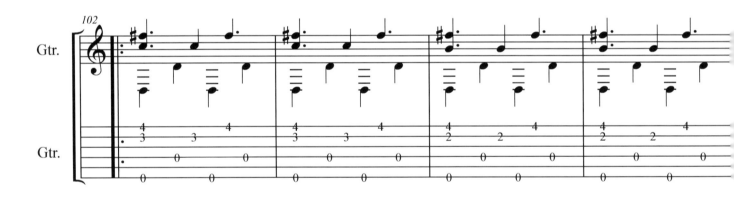

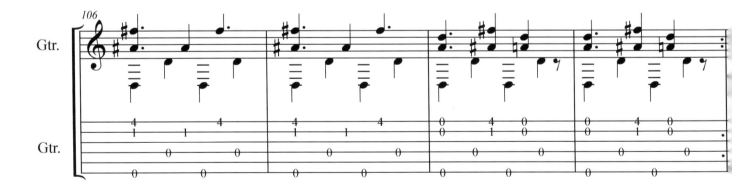

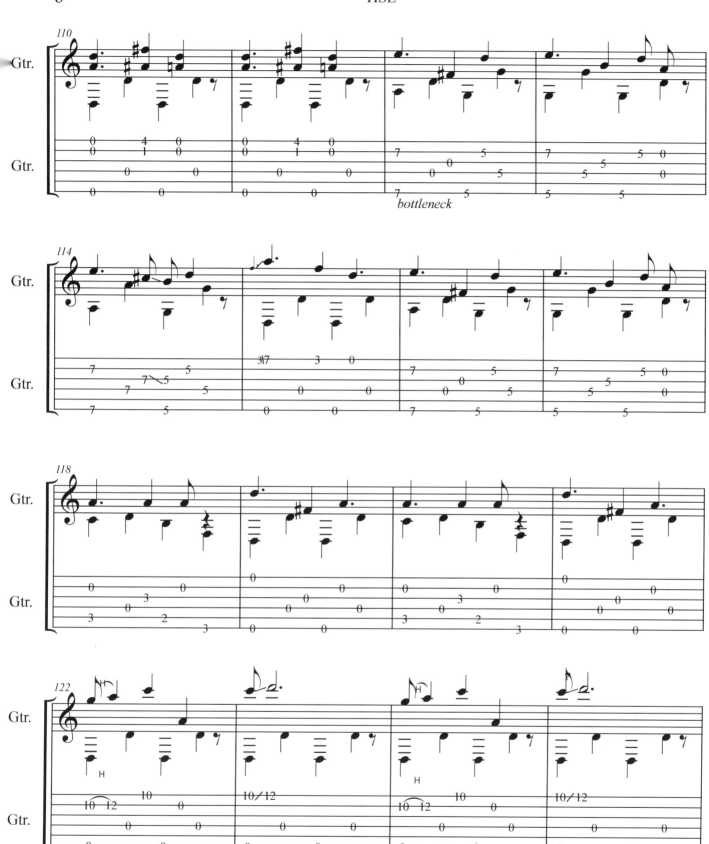

bottleneck

HSE

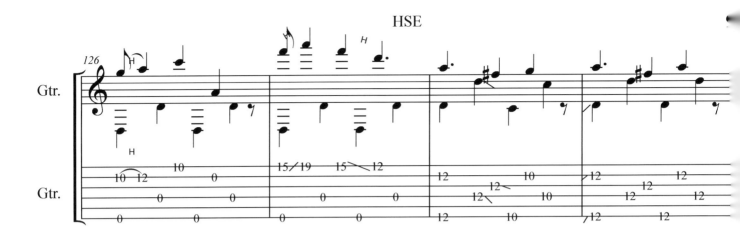

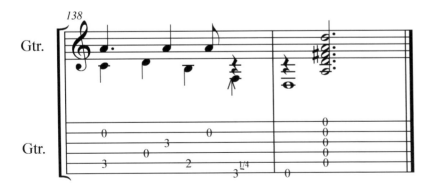

103

# CHAPTER 4:
## DROPPED D TUNING

*In this chapter we will:*

*• Learn to play two fingepicked songs in dropped-D tuning: "Badlands" and "Going Down to Richmond."*

# INTRODUCTION TO DROPPED-D TUNING

In a way dropped-D tuning provides the best of both worlds: you get the low droning quality of the 6th string D note, combined with the ability to work the rest of the string in standard tuning. Of course, this is only helpful if you know your fretboard fairly well.

There is only one change to be made in dropped D: lower the 6th string from E to D. You can use this low string as a drone, or as an alternating D/D bass with the 4th string, or as a monotonic/ "dead" thumb bass.

The two original compositions presented here work the fretboard a bit. "Badlands" is a framework upon which you can hang your slow, evocative slide lines; its meant to have a brooding quality.

"Goin' Down to Richmond" is also a slower, solo piece. It is somewhat inspired by the playing of Ry Cooder. I use the open D string(s) to create a drone effect In the first 48 bars its actually better to not have the slide on your finger. Then, in the second section, placing the bottleneck on your finger to get the minimalistic slide notes.

# Badlands

Dropped D tuning:
DADGBE

**Pete Madsen**

"Badlands" is another dropped-D composition that is centered around an A-shaped D minor chord. The opening sequence (first 4 bars) is mainly about using the 4th and 6th strings as drone notes and then at the end of the repeat on the 4th bar we chromatically walk into a partial A-shaped D minor chord. This section is surrounded by ascending and descending chromatic runs. We then play an E-shaped G7 chord, but again the low bass note has to be fretted two frets up from normal because of the 6th string being lowered. We descend from this chord down to an F, then an E and Eb that uses open strings. This section finishes off with an E-shaped Fmajor7th chord and repeats back to the beginning.

After the second pass through we end up at bar 16 where we employ a higher voiced version of the D minor we were playing in measures 5-9. This eight bar section uses a G-shape G chord with notes that descend on the 4th and 5th strings (measures 17 and 21); an E-shape A and G chords (measure 19) and the same E and Eb chords form the previous section. We then play one more pass through this eight bar section but with an improvisational aspect. I use the D minor measure to play licks based on minor pentatonic scales.

2

4

Tempo
Practice: 80 bpm
Performance: 112 bpm

# Goin' Down to Richmond

**Pete Madsen**

This is an original tune meant to played in the style of Ry Cooder. It has a swampy groove that uses a "dead" thumb bass in dropped D tuning (DADGBE). About a third of the way in comes a bottleneck slide guitar line that stays until the end of the song.

   The opening 8 bars are a drone of sorts: lots of low "D" notes. The second section, beginning at bar 9 has a call and response quality to it: these phrases are built on 4 bar sections - the first three bars are the "call" and the last bar has a varied response. The last 4 bar section is broken into a two bar call and a two bar response. An exercise for the motivated student would be to come up with a few more responses to the call. In measure 25 we move into a section that splits between an alternating bass and borrowing a part of the intro. The phrase in measure 41-42 is a little difficult and involves hammer-on notes over open strings - listen carefully to the recording to get the phrasing correct. Immediately following is a phrase that involves fretting the 6th string bass while you play harmonics. I use my pinky to sound the harmonics, but you can use any finger that works for you.

On page 4 we begin a section that uses the bottleneck. At measure 48 you let the low D note sustain. This gives you time to put the slide on your finger and play. If you are wondering why you don't start with the bottleneck on it's because the earlier passages require that all your fingers on your left hand be free; otherwise the fingerings would be very difficult. This section uses a dead-thumb bass with some very minimalistic slide lines.

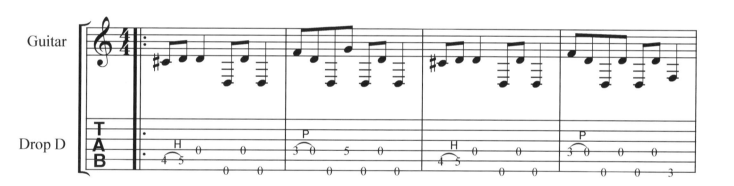

Goin Down to Richmond

Place bottleneck slide on finger

113

Goin Down to Richmond

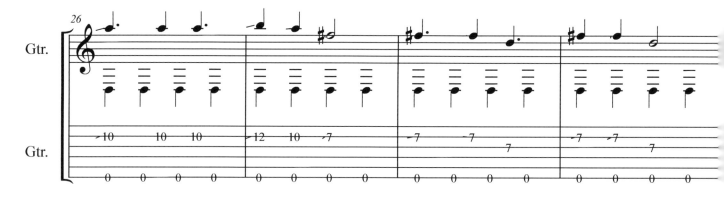

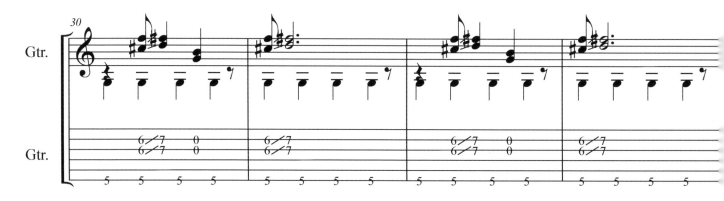

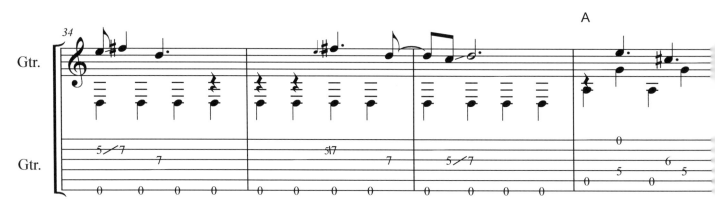

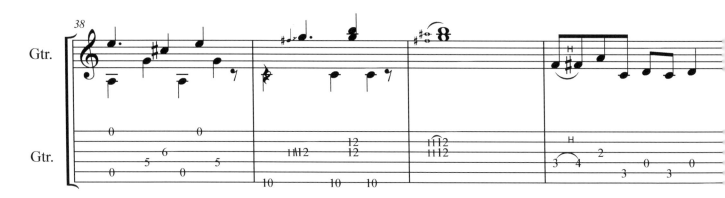

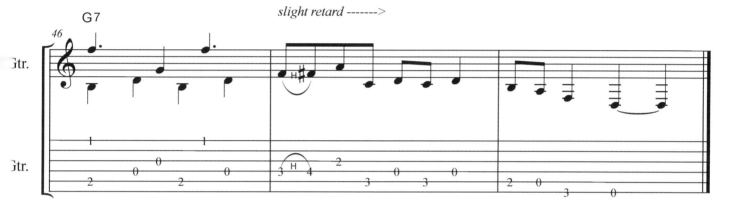

# CHAPTER 5: STANDARD TUNING

*In this chapter we will:*

• *We will learn some scales and licks in the key of E.*

• *Learn a slow blues groove in E*

• *Learn two twelve bar solos to go along with the slow groove in E*

• *Play a "Statesboro Blues-style" groove and play a solo that combines slide licks with non-slide licks in the key of G.*

• *Learn the rhythm and melody line to the song "Sleepwalk."*

# INTRODUCTION TO STANDARD TUNING

 When I play slide in standard tuning I am always accompanied by another player or band – it's harder to keep any kind of steady bass going. So all the playing examples in this chapter will have two guitar parts: rhythm and lead.

What works for non-slide soloing in standard tuning also works for slide; namely, scales, riffs and chord shapes.


## Soloing:

I tell my students to think of their solos as having a conversational quality: a call and response. Your solos will sound more interesting if you try to emulate everyday speech. If you listen to people's conversations you will hear exclamations, questions, laughter, anger, playfulness and, most of all, pauses. Think of your solo as being a dialogue between two people (I know that sounds a little schitzophrenic, but if you maintain just this one aspect to your solo playing you will never be boring! Conversely, if you sound like you are playing non-stop scale tones with no pauses, inflections or dynamics, people will tune you out real quick).

## Exercises and licks:

The following exercises and licks are derived from minor pentatonic scales and will be played mostly on the first two strings. We will play an ascending E minor pentatonic scale on the first and second strings. With your slide on you should try to aim for the actual fret wire, rather than in between the frets, to achieve proper intonation. Try sliding between each note of the scale, ascending and then descending.

How does it sound? Check your intonation by fretting the notes with your finger and then the slide. Do they sound the same? or does the slide note sound a little flat? If so, try to target right over the fret wire.

Lick 1: On the surface this lick is pretty simple: play an open string and then slide into the notes of an ascending pentatonic scale. However, there is a trick with the damping finger I would like you to try. In general, the damping finger should be the first thing to touch the string and the last thing you remove. If you play this lick and don't use a damping finger you will notice that you will get a "ghost" pull-off sound. You may say, "I like that sound," but if its not intentional its going to be there whether you like it or not.

Lick 2: The same thing can be said for lick 2: you play an open 2nd string followed by a slide on the 3rd fret and then the same thing on the first string. Try to keep track of your damping finger.

Lick 3: This lick uses a descending slide lick that moves between the 2nd - 3rd strings and then ascends on the 4th string to resolve on an E note. Try to lift your slide and keep the damping finger down as you move from string to string.

Lick 4: This one uses a slide on the 2nd string which alternates with the open 1st string and then resolves with the previous lick (lick 3).

Lick 5: In this lick if you took just the last three notes you would have an E minor triad, but I have added the 2nd degree of an E minor scale to give this lick a slightly different flavor. Moving between strings can be little challenging with the slide. As you move from the 1st to the second string try starting out with the slide slightly tilted outward from the fretboard. Then tilt the slide inwards as you progress to the 2nd and then 3rd strings.

Lick 6: This lick covers the same fretboard territory as lick 5 but is focused on the "inner" strings (2-4). You don't need to tilt your slide for this lick. Try keeping the slide very straight, covering all the strings.

Lick 7: This lick moves up to the 12th fret and beyond up to the 15th fret. You may need to slant your slide to get up to the 15th fret, but that's okay as long as you are only targeting the one string (Note: when playing multiple strings at the same time be careful that your slide is not slanted and that it lines up perfectly with the fret, otherwise you will sound out of tune.)

Lick 8: Lick 8 is also centered at the 12th fret but we play a backwards slide from the 15th fret to get there.

Lick 9: Here we use a chromatic run to move from the 12th to the 15th fret. Sometimes you will want to use the slide to play non-affected notes, but then slide into another note. So we will simply use the slide to cover the string and pluck the notes at the 12th, 13th and 14th frets on the 2nd string; then slide into the D note at the 15th fret.

Lick 10: We can also use the slide to play slightly sharp or flat notes. In this lick as you slide on the 2nd string from the 10th fret up to the 12th fret you can let the slide ascend a little as you play the slightly sharpened E note on the 12th fret of the 1st string. This produces a slightly unresolved and haunting sound. The same idea is used in the 2nd measure of this phrase as we slide backwards 12th to the 11th fret on the 2nd string.

Slow Blues Groove and Solos:

I have given you a slow 12 bar, 3 chord groove in E to play some solos with. The groove is a variation on a basic shuffle. We play a two beat two string chord followed by a single beat E6 and 8th note triplet — this riff dominates the groove throughout. There is a lot of space in the rhythm for you to play through with your slide.

There are two 12 bar solos. The first solo uses a repeating lick that is anchored by an E note played at the 5th fret on the 2nd string. As the lick progresses it resolves to an A note in the 5th measure which is when the rhythm shifts to the A chord. We also play the root note of the B chord with the slide when the rhythm moves to B in measure 9.

In the second 12 bar solo we move up to the 12th fret, but use a similar rhythmic phrasing as the first few bars of the previous 12 bar. In measure 15 we perform a Duane Allman-style lick in which we slide quickly backwards on the first string from the 12th to the 10th fret and ascend up a little slower on the 2nd string from the 10-12th fret. Measures 16-18 pulls notes from a the middle range of the guitar. We then work our way down to a lower range. We finish off with a lick that starts on the 1st string and works its way up the fretboard to play an E minor triad between measure 22-23.

# Slide in Standard Tuning: Key of E

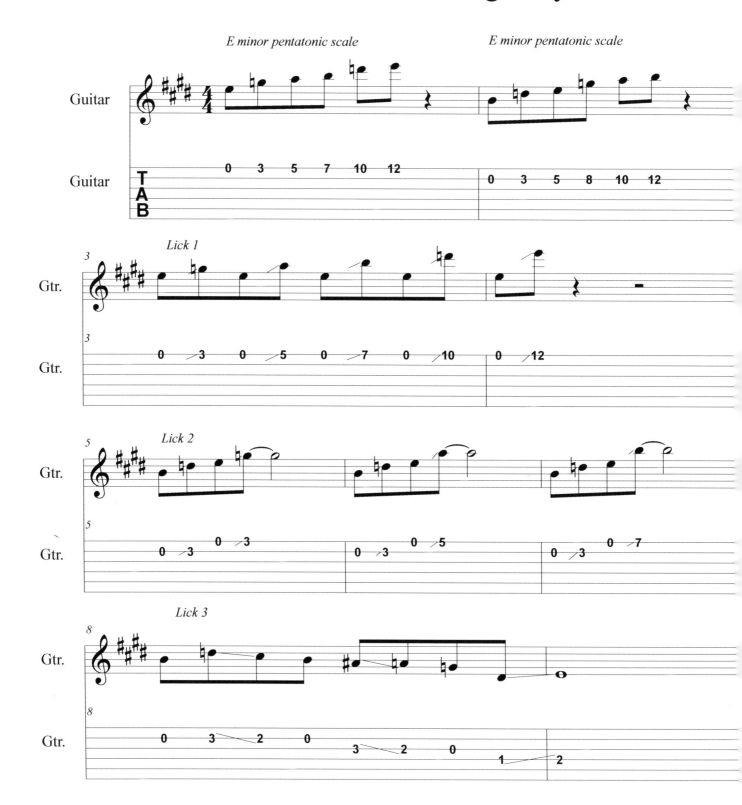

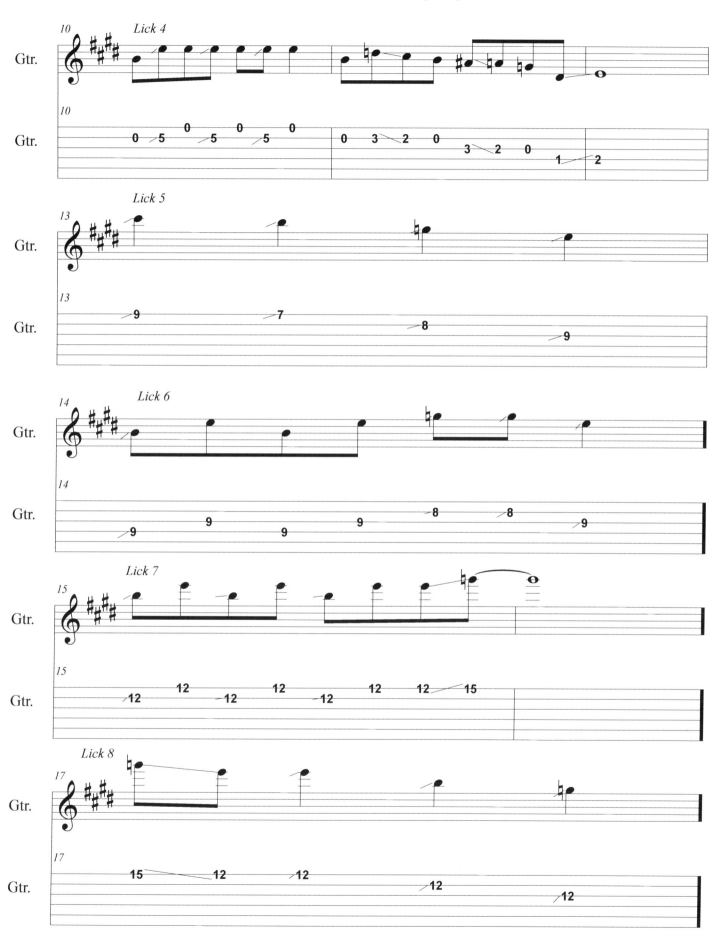

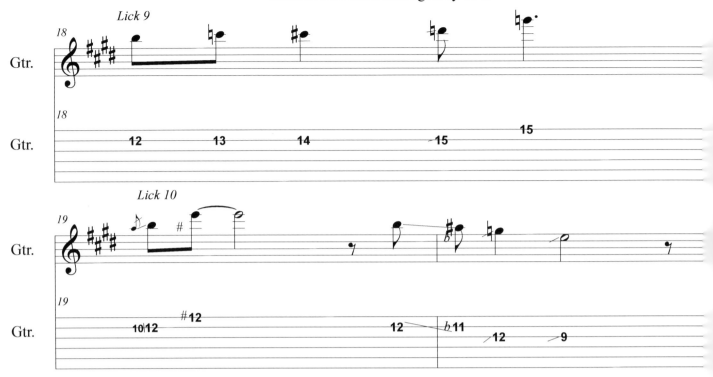

# Slow Blues in E Groove

# Slide Solos in Standard Tuning: E 12 bar

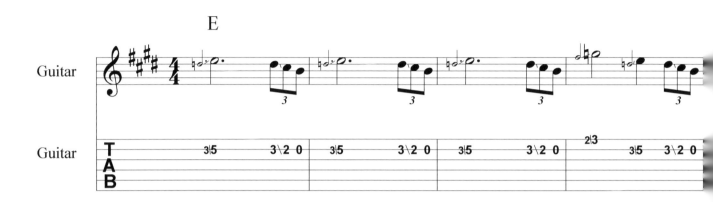

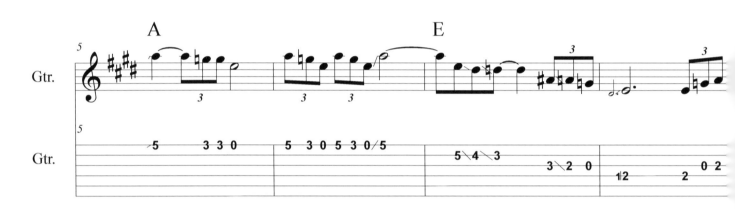

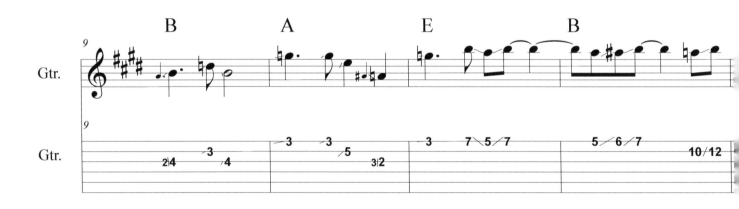

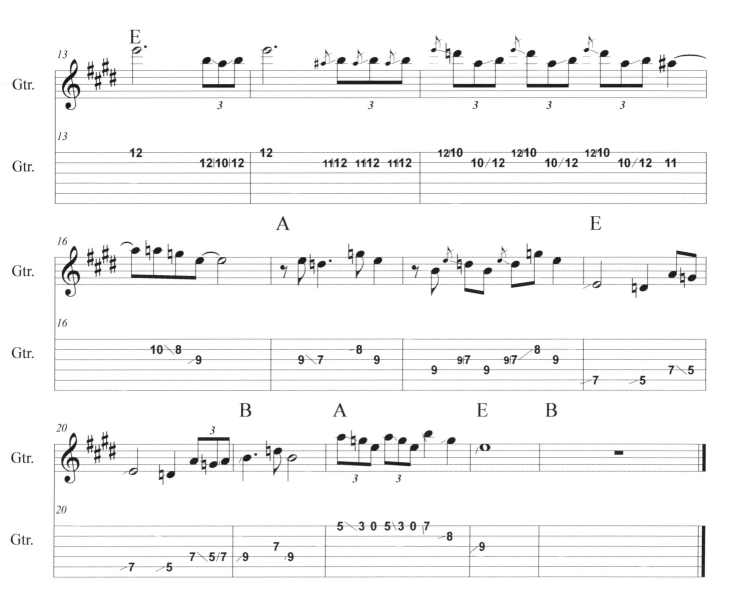

# Statesboro Groove w/slide/no slide
## Standard Tuning: EADGBE

Playing in standard tuning is a good opportunity to combine slide licks with no-slide licks. This 12 bar blues in G works through three verses and uses double-stops, hammer-ons and slide licks.

    The first verse starts with a double-stop that hints at a G7 chord. We then play a slide lick based on a first position G minor pentatonic scale. Come back to the original double-stop and then play another slide lick based out of a 2nd position G minor pentatonic punctuated by a double-stop slide lick played at the 12th fret on the 3rd and 4th strings – remember that the 2nd, 3rd and 4th strings are tuned the same in standard tuning as open G tuning; so you actually have a full G major triad on those three strings. In measure 9, at the 7th fret we play a partial D chord with the slide.

    The second verse is centered around a triplet hammer-on lick that we will repeat throughout. We will also use this same lick, played an octave higher, in the third verse. In bar 22 we use a chromatic lick to work up to the 12 fret and finish with the slide there.

    In the third verse we start where we ended the second verse – at the 12th fret; then play the hammer-on riff at the 15-18th frets. In bars 28-29 we will use the G note on the 1st string/15th as a pedal tone and descend on the second string. In bar 34 we play an oblique bend that is followed by a series of descending pull-offs.

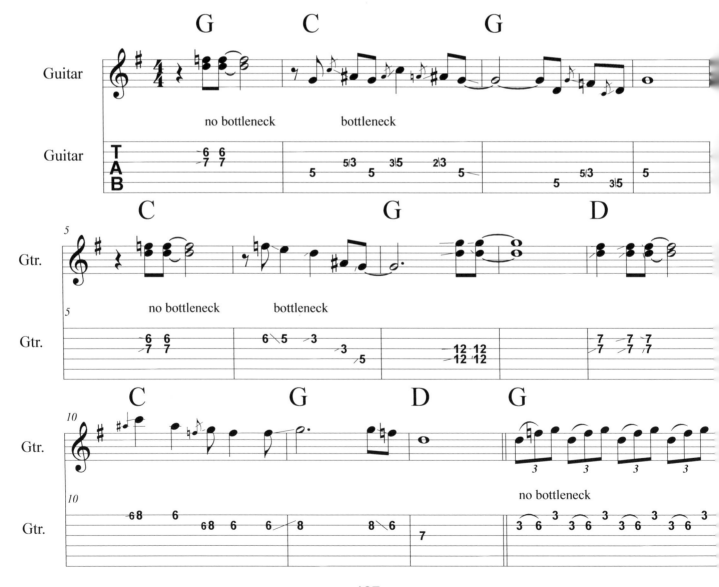

Statesboro Groove w/slide/no slide

# Sleepwalk rhythm

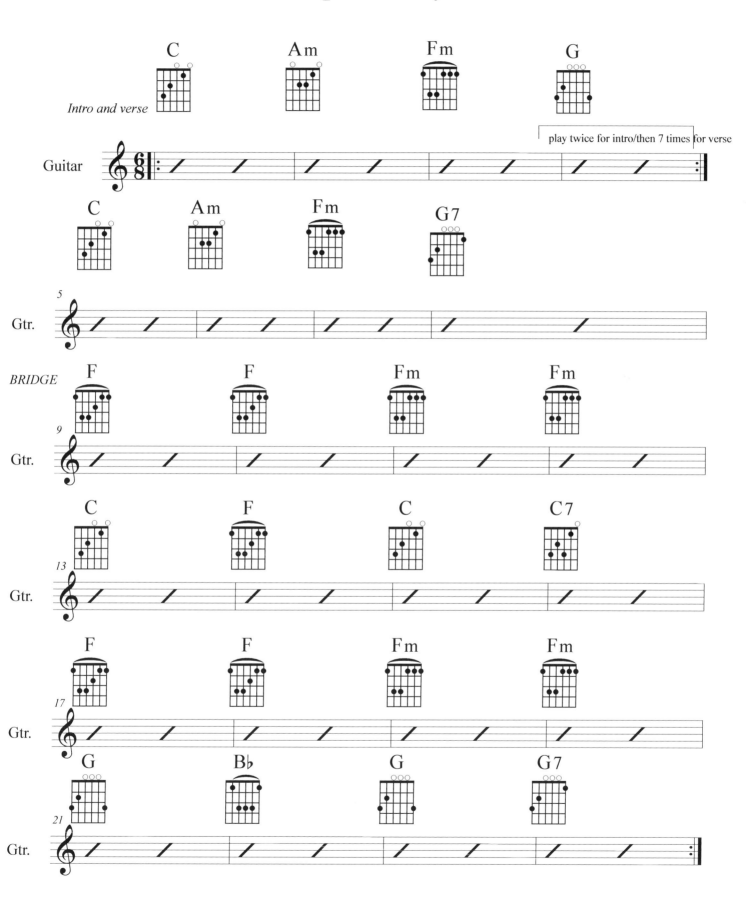

# Sleepwalk -- melody

Santo and Johnny

Pete Madsen

*Play with bottleneck throughout*

Sleepwalk -- melody

FOUR MEASURE IMPROVISATION OVER C-F-C-C7

# CHAPTER 6:
## OTHER TUNINGS

*In this chapter we will:*

• *Learn about C tuning and play the song "Watermelon Seeds."*

• *Learn about D7 tuning and play the song "Le Petit Nicolas."*

# Watermelon seeds

Open C Tuning:
C G C G C E

**Pete Madsen**

This song was inspired by Leo Kottke's song "Watermelon," from his great album 6 and 12 String Guitar - sometimes called the "Armadillo" album because of the picture of the scaly creature on the cover. Kottke's tune was in a lowered version of Open D tuning and played on the 12 string. "Watermelon Seeds" is in open C tuning (CGCGCE) and I've played it both on 12 and 6 string guitars.

The opening is a mood setter with open chord strums combined with multiple string slide strums. Then the A section sets a quick pace which is sustained for the rest of the song - this section is played with an "almost" alternating bass pattern. The B section is a true alternating bass with slide notes played on the first string. A later version of this same section uses harmonics instead of slide notes. Other than that it's pretty straight forward.

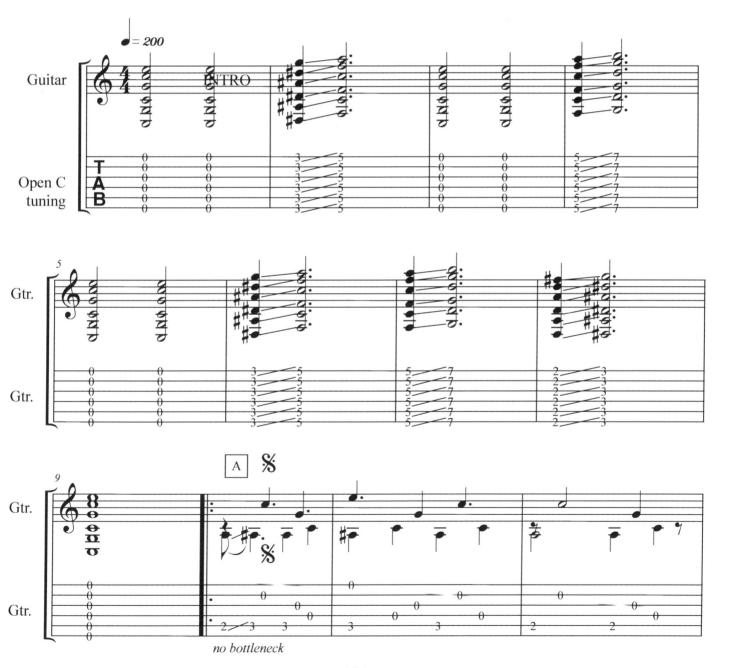

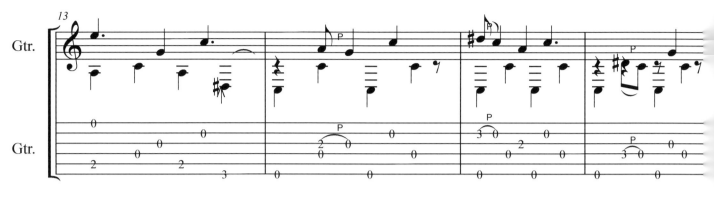

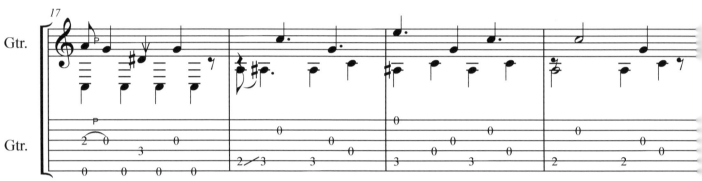

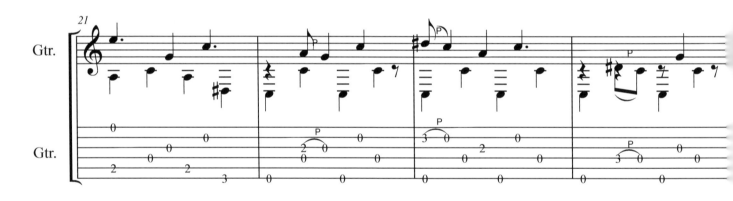

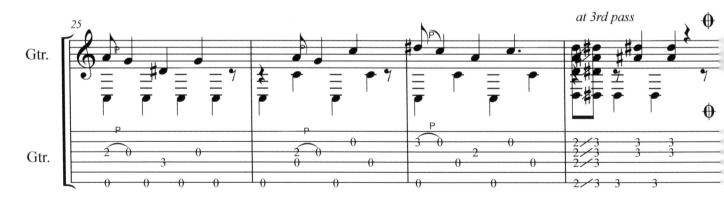

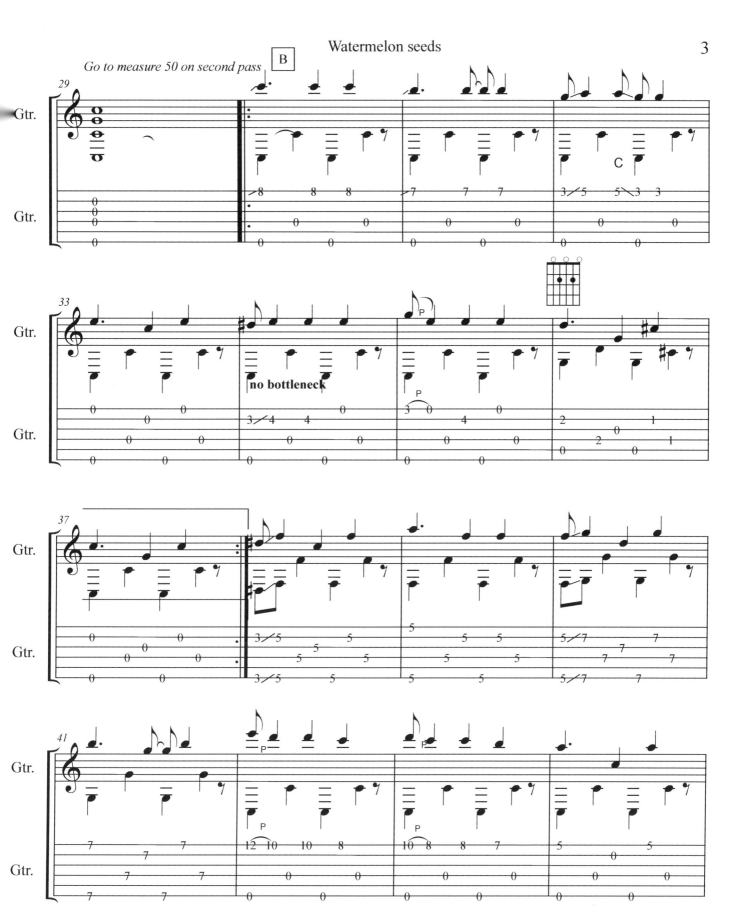

Watermelon seeds

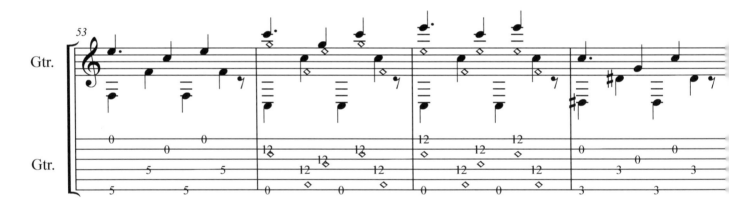

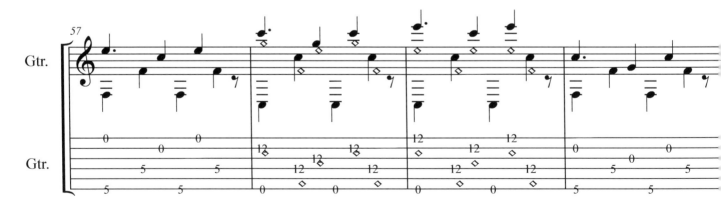

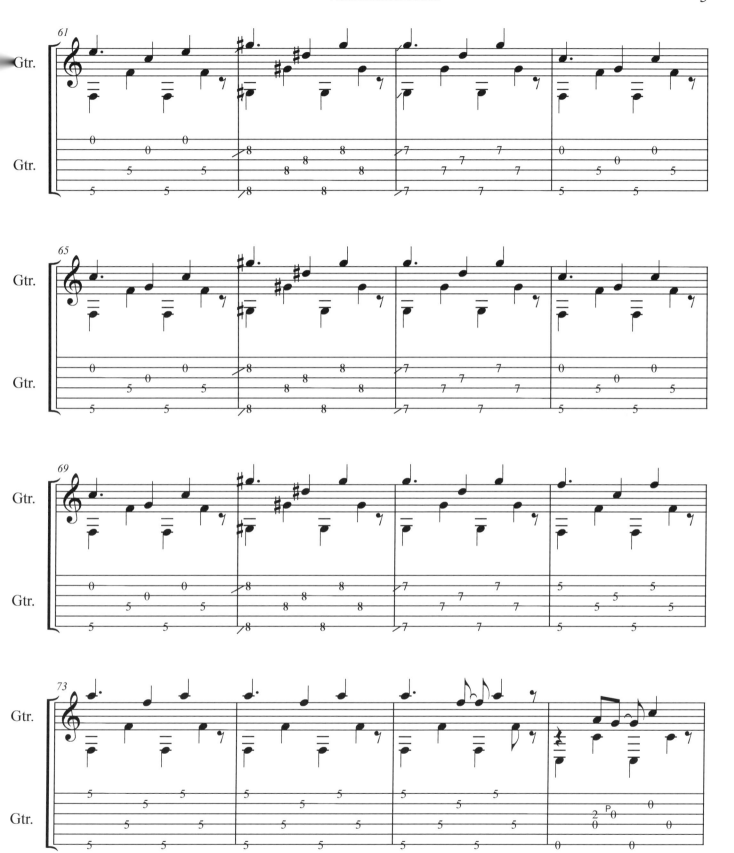

Watermelon seeds

# Le Petit Nicolas

### D7 Tuning: D-A-D-F#-C-D

**Pete**

This one is a little different. It's in D7 tuning, which is variation of open D tuning. The only difference between the two is that in D7 tuning the 2nd string is tuned to C instead of A. So your tuning for this song will be:

```
6   5   4   3   2   1
D↓  A   D   F#↓ C   D↓
```

Right from the get go we have some odd stuff going on. The opening lick is executed by "bouncing" the slide on the first string at the 1st fret. It helps if your slide is of the heavier variety. Also, make sure that your thumb is securely on the back of the neck of your guitar so that you have a stable perch from which to bounce. You then play an arabic-sounding scale with the slide which culminates with a series of barred chords (use your slide) and a lick that is described below.

*Note 1:* To play this lick you first want to play a harmonic on the 1st string/12th fret. Then you take your slide and place it behind the nut where you will "roll" over the nut as you come back in contact with the string. From there you can get a series of "slid" notes up the neck.

From measures 11-26 we play a series of "snapped" bass notes followed by multi-string slides. The snapping involves taking your thumb or pick under the 6th string and pulling it away from the guitar, thus yielding a "popping" sound.

We then move into a section that is dominated by an alternating bass pattern, chords that are fully barred by the slide and and some nice bell-like harmonics played at the 12th fret.

Starting in measure 70 we move into what I like to call the "quirky" section. This sections starts out with a series of rolling hammer-ons — I use my index finger to hammer-on the 6th string and my ring finger to play the 4th string. In measure 74 we switch to a series of pull-offs which should be fingered by the thumb on the 6th string and the index finger on the first string.

INTRO: Arabic sounding; free time
Tempo: 168bpm

2

Le Petit Nicolas

Le Petit Nicolas

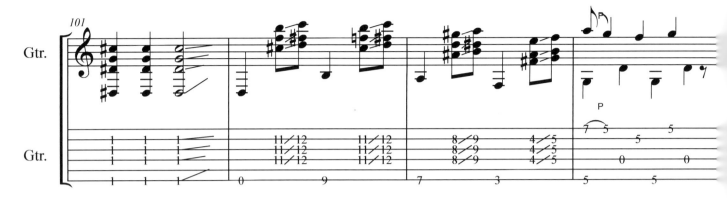

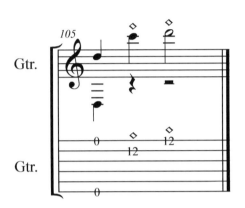

# TAB Ex

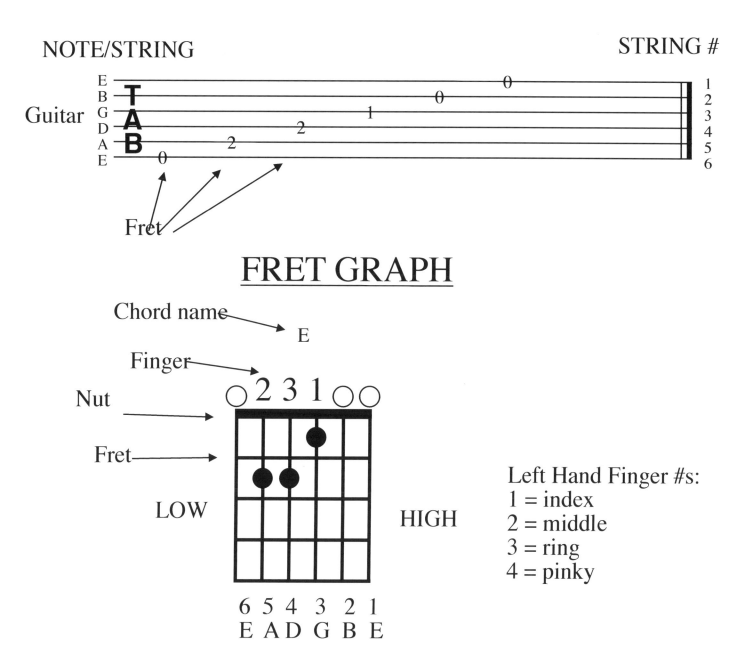

The two illustrations above represent a measue of TAB and a
FRET GRAPH. TAB is musical notation specifically for the
guitar. Each line represents a string, from 1 (Hi E) to 6 (low E). The
numbers represented on each line tell you which FRET to play. The
FRET GRAPH is like a picture of the guitar fretboard. In this example it
is telling you where to put your fingers to make an E chord

148

# TAB legend

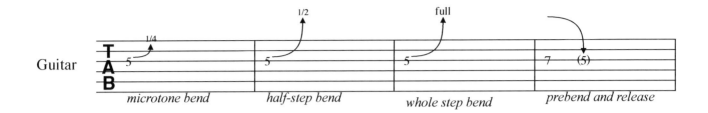

Guitar

microtone bend     half-step bend     whole step bend     prebend and release

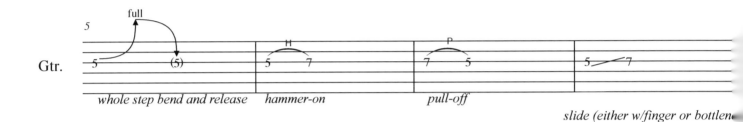

Gtr.

whole step bend and release     hammer-on     pull-off

slide (either w/finger or bottlen●

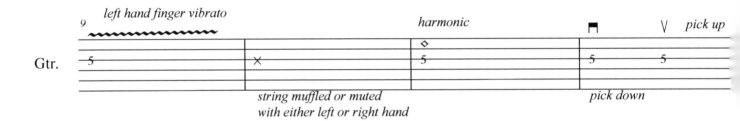

Gtr.

left hand finger vibrato     harmonic     pick up

string muffled or muted
with either left or right hand     pick down

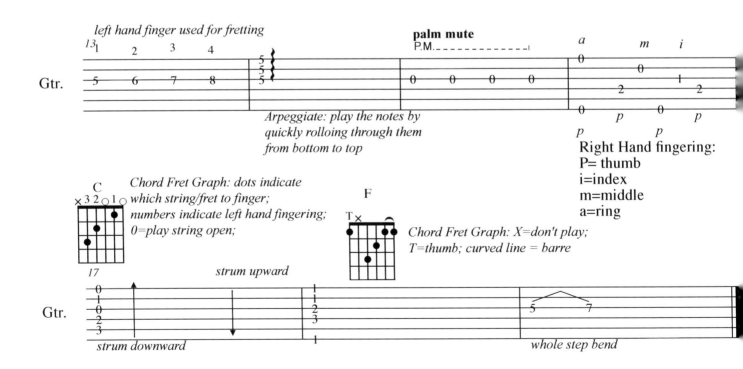

Gtr.

left hand finger used for fretting     palm mute     P.M.

Arpeggiate: play the notes by
quickly rolloing through them
from bottom to top

Right Hand fingering:
P= thumb
i=index
m=middle
a=ring

C

Chord Fret Graph: dots indicate
which string/fret to finger;
numbers indicate left hand fingering;
0=play string open;

F

Chord Fret Graph: X=don't play;
T=thumb; curved line = barre

strum upward

Gtr.

strum downward     whole step bend

Printed in Great Britain
by Amazon